Illinois Central College
Learning Resources Center

GAYLORD

The Films of Woody Allen is the first full-length critical study of Woody Allen to analyze in depth the films that make Allen a serious filmmaker and artist. Sam Girgus argues that Allen is on the cutting edge of contemporary critical and cultural consciousness, challenging our notions of authorship, narrative, perspective, character, theme, ideology, gender, and sexuality. A student and admirer of the classic Hollywood cinema, Allen combines this appreciation for American directors with a developed sensitivity to experimental European directors such as Fellini, De Sica, and Bergman. Probably the most widely recognized aspect of Allen's work is his uncanny integration of the comedic and the serious in visually inventive films that experiment with narrative, plot, and psychology. Beginning with *Play It Again, Sam,* the films of Woody Allen offer a perceptive vision of contemporary life and the human condition. The increasing complexity of his works as a director and writer over two decades has paralleled an equally complex process of intellectual and moral maturity. Allen's films reveal a decentered world of displaced and dislocated characters who question their ability to find meaning in their lives. Allen's achievement as an artist has been to develop a style of technical and artistic complexity to sustain his vision.

The Films of Woody Allen

CAMBRIDGE FILM CLASSICS

General Editor: Raymond Carney, Boston University

Other books in the series:

The Films of
Woody Allen

SAM B. GIRGUS

Vanderbilt University

CAMBRIDGE
UNIVERSITY PRESS

Published by the Press Syndicate of the University of Cambridge
The Pitt Building, Trumpington Street, Cambridge CB2 1RP
40 West 20th Street, New York, NY 10011-4211, USA
10 Stamford Road, Oakleigh, Victoria 3166, Australia

First published 1993

Printed in the United States of America

Library of Congress Cataloging-in-Publication Data
Girgus, Sam B., 1941–
The films of Woody Allen / Sam B. Girgus.
p.   cm. – (Cambridge film classics)
Filmography: p.
ISBN 0-521-38095-2 (hardback). – ISBN 0-521-38999-2 (paperback)
1. Allen, Woody – Criticism and interpretation.   I. Title.   II. Series.
PN1998.3.A45G7   1993
791.43′092–dc20   92-23020
CIP

A catalog record for this book is available from the British Library

ISBN 0-521-38095-2   hardback
0-521-38999-2   paperback

To Scottie

Contents

Preface

His inner life has always been there on the screen for all to see. His most intense yearnings and desires have been played out in his movies for almost a generation. The merging of art and reality, normality and neurosis, has comprised the core of his films. The testing of taboos and prohibitions and the craving for impossible love have been pervasive. Thus, the scandal that erupted when Woody Allen's private life became public earlier this month should not have been a surprise, no matter how much we laughed at his humor, empathized with his characters, and loved him for his brilliance and originality. Because Allen's personal tragedy and crisis fulfill themes, drives, and motifs that permeate his work, everyone should have anticipated it: critics, admirers, skeptics. Nevertheless, the explosion of scandal and pain could not help but shock us and undoubtedly will influence our perception of his work. At the same time, this extraordinary collapse of the public and private makes the wish to study his work in depth even more compelling. His own journey through moral and emotional crisis finds a parallel in the ever-deepening moral complexity and ambiguity of his work. Even more than we realized, a critical and interpretative study of Allen's films clearly also entails the construction of an interior biography of him.

Although the stories and publicity about Allen's personal relationships and domestic turmoil broke when the following study was finished and in page proofs, these events do not change in any radical way the interpretation of Allen and his work. They do suggest, however, that with Allen the jokes and the humor, as we thought, really were serious. In his life as in his films, darkness and light commingle to present a complex rendering of experience. It is impossible to predict with certainty what recent events portend for Allen's career and work – or, for that matter, what they will mean for those people, young and old, associated with him. What we can suggest, however, is that media, public, and critical reaction to this "breaking story" has dramatized how important Allen and his films have become to our critical and cultural consciousness. In the following pages, I hope to offer some insights into the artistic achievement and cultural significance of several of these films and to explain why they speak so forcefully to so many of our concerns today.

August 1992

Acknowledgments

Karen Stenard, Susan Tate, Trey Harwell, and James Earl helped me with this manuscript, and I would like to thank them for their time and effort. Emory Elliott, Sacvan Bercovitch, and Robet Sklar continue to provide great support and friendship. Ray Carney and Beatrice Rehl of this film series at Cambridge University Press have been especially encouraging. Over the years, the list of students, colleagues, and friends at various universities and institutions who have provided friendship and support has grown almost too long to mention. At Vanderbilt, I would especially like to thank Paul Elledge, Cecelia Tichi, Paul Conkin, Nancy Walker, Ann Cook, Chris Hassel, Margaret Doody, Laurence Lerner, William Engel, Sam McSeveney, John Halperin, Michael Kreyling, Jay Clayton, Margaret Bass, Valerie Traub, Robert Mack, Phyllis Frus, Vivien Fryd, and Marilyn Murphy for their encouragement as my work moves toward film studies and American culture. Friends and colleagues from overseas also have greeted the idea of hearing about Woody Allen and film with enthusiasm: Viola Sachs, Yassen Zassoursky, Nadia Khromchenko, Ellen Spolsky, Cristina Giorcelli, Avner Ziv, Andreas Hofele, Mike Parker, Itala Vivan, Dieter Schulz, Sharon Baris, Maya Koreneva, Daniel Garcia, Claudia Banis-Suermann.

Former colleagues from New Mexico keep telling me what I need to know about films, Hollywood, humor, and life in general: Ham Hill and Arlette Hill, Joel Jones and Nancy Magnuson, Mary Bess Whidden and Angela Boone, Peter White, Helen Damico, Lee Bartlett, Robert Fleming, Gary Scharnhorst, David McPherson. I know I speak for all of them when I say how much we will miss the wisdom, wit, and warmth of George Arms and the compassion and care of our former chairman, Joe Zavadil.

The patience and support of students and friends seemed inexhaustible as they helped me learn about cinema studies and American studies: Robert

Johnstone, Jane Ritter, Louise Bishop, Elizabeth Fox-Genovese, Richard Brown, Lucy Fischer, Judith Fryer, Leonard Kriegel, John Cawelti, Alan Trachtenberg, Art Wrobel, Ed Hotaling, Bill Jones, J. Delayney Barber, Charles Walker, Phil Burnham, Annie Eysturoy, Magda Zaborowska, Zsuzsa Nemeth, Michele Conte, Tony Piccolo, Skip Daube, Brian Jones, Colleen Kelley, Ann McDonald, Caroline Woidat, Lisa Seifker-Long, Marilyn Allison, Derah Myers, Ted Mulvaney, and Gary Richards. To be fair, I should include all the students in film courses during the past two years at Vanderbilt who have been such a special joy and pleasure to teach.

Finally, my greatest thanks goes, as always, to the source of my greatest support and love, Scottie and our daughters – Katya, Meighan, and Jennifer – my mother, as well as Aida, Audrey, Harris, and our growing family members: Ali, Danny, Negi, Jeff. To all of them, my love and appreciation.

I
Reconstruction and Revision in Woody Allen's films

Vincent Canby consistently hails him as our most important comedic director. Pauline Kael regularly assails him as predictable and self-indulgent. Other critics such as Terrence Rafferty sometimes express disappointment over his efforts, but still acknowledge the special quality and character of his work. To both the popular press and serious students of cinema, Woody Allen seems to be an eccentric and enigmatic genius who works with integrity as an innovative artist in an industry and medium dominated by commercial interests and mass tastes. Moreover, other directors now imitate him in ways that suggest Allen's elevation as an influence and a force among that special group of critics, one's peers. For example, Rob Reiner promoted one of his own films as a kind of tribute to Allen's unique style, whereas Spike Lee's narrative voice and innovative directing in recent films often reflect Allen's work.

Because he is a celebrity and part of a world of mass entertainment, Allen's true artistic achievement and significance are easily minimized. This is unfortunate because Allen's work should be studied with the same close attention given to other serious artists and writers. While books about Allen and his work have accumulated steadily over the years, few detailed studies of the artistry of the individual films have appeared. On the cutting edge of contemporary critical and cultural consciousness, Allen challenges most of our traditional notions of authorship, narrative, perspective, character development, theme, ideology, gender construction, and sexuality. A student and admirer of the classic Hollywood cinema of the 1930s and 1940s, Allen combines this appreciation for American directors with a developed sensitivity to experimental European directors such as Federico Fellini, Vittorio De Sica, and most important, Ingmar Bergman. These diverse interests form the artistry of his own movies. Probably the most widely recognized aspect of Allen's work involves his integration of the comedic and serious in visually inventive films that experiment with narrative sequence, multiple plots, intense psychological character studies, and urbane sophistication. At the same time, the ever-increasing complexity of his work as a director and writer over the past 20 years has paralleled an equally complex process of intellectual and moral maturation. Since *Play It Again, Sam,* the films of Woody Allen proffer an important vision of contemporary life and the human condition. His films reveal a decentered world of displaced and dislocated characters who question their ability to find meaning in their lives. His achievement as an artist has been to develop a style of technical and artistic complexity to sustain this vision.

It is accurate and useful to note that Woody Allen has become a legend in his own times. His face appears on countless magazine covers. Stories and legends about him abound. In fact, myth and reality about Woody Allen merge to create an intriguing and extraordinary figure. He was born Allen Stewart Konigsberg on December 1, 1935, and grew up in the lower-middle-class area of Flatbush, Brooklyn.[1] His background and upbringing were Jewish, and his movies reflect the enormous influence of ethnic cultures on his way of thinking, feeling, and creating. His father, Martin, had many different jobs ranging from jewelry engraving to bartending, while his mother, Nettie, was a bookkeeper for a Brooklyn florist. He attended public schools and was generally a mediocre student. As a youngster he was interested in sports and girls; but as a teenager attending Midwood High School in Brooklyn, he developed an obsession with writing gag lines and submitting them to newspaper columnists and writers such as Earl Wilson, who used them. Such acceptance of his work marked the meager beginnings of his career as a comic and humorist. He was less successful as a college student, entering and quickly leaving both City College and New York University. College seemed relatively unimportant to him, as he achieved early success as a full-time comic writer for major comedians, Sid Caesar, Buddy Hackett, and Jack Paar, and important shows, including "The Tonight Show" and "Your Show of Shows." According to Douglas Brode, at the age of 22, Allen was earning as much as $1,500 a week by writing gags for Garry Moore's popular television program. Partly because of his high regard for Mort Sahl, whose political humor was in great demand during the early sixties, Allen's success as a gag writer gave him the confidence to attempt his own comic routine. His stand-up comedy not only helped to establish his public reputation; it also gave him the opportunity to develop his relationship with the two agents who have worked with him throughout his career, Charles H. Joffe and Jack Rollins. From his tentative and awkward beginnings as a stand-up comic in offbeat New York clubs such as The Bitter End, Allen eventually triumphed in the biggest clubs in Las Vegas and New York and on the most popular television programs of the time.

As Allen's work developed in sophistication, his humorous stories also appeared regularly in the *New Yorker* and *Playboy* and were later collected as extremely popular books: *Without Feathers, Getting Even,* and *Side Effects.* His greatest popularity, however, came with the success of his films. Some fans and critics continue to insist that his earliest films are his funniest and most original. His first film was *What's New, Pussycat?* in 1965, which appropriately enough was backed by someone who had been impressed by his stand-up performance at the Blue Angel. This film was followed by several others that indicate an initial zany phase to his film career that lasted through 1971 with *Bananas.* In between there was *What's Up, Tiger Lily?, Casino Royale, Don't Drink the Water,* and *Take the Money and Run.*

Allen's popularity and success in these films are extensions of his earlier success. In retrospect, during these stages of his career, Allen seems perfectly suited to his times. The sixties, we recall, was a period of enormous social and cultural revolution, entailing changes whose ultimate impact still remains uncertain today. For the older generation, this was a time of nearly unbelievable sexual revolution marked by a troubling and paradoxical contradiction in general between forces of skepticism and cynicism, on the one hand, and forces of idealism and hope, on the other. The mingling of these forces during this Vietnam War era naturally exacerbated confusion and tension. In a time of democratic upheaval that touched all aspects of life from the sexual and social to the cultural and political, Allen's looks and offbeat style seemed to speak for and represent the involvement of "everyman" in the transformations of life-styles and values. His persona as a "loser," the classic underdog "schlemiel" figure, was perfect for a period of participatory democracy and confusing change, but also allowed for a process of distancing from developments and events that contained frightening potential within them. One could look at and listen to Woody Allen and identify with him, while also feeling somewhat estranged from him.

It also was the period of Martin Luther King and the black revolution, which began a new form of ethnic turmoil and controversy for our country that also remains with us today. Allen's ethnicity highlights this phenomenon of racial and cultural difference in a nonthreatening way. Indeed, the general absence of blacks or people of color from his films may in some ways imply a lingering tension in his work over this issue. In addition, the sixties was a student- and campus-centered period. Allen's wit and playfulness embodied the combination of sophistication and experimental innocence that characterizes youth in general, but this period in particular. Allen catered to a generation and public that were receptive to and ready for his artful manipulation of and experimentation with language and visual images. The first generation in history to be raised on the modern media revolution, it was acclimated to a multimedia, global village cultural environment. Accustomed to tumultuous events and times that were brought home to them through the new immediacy of modern media, this audience and public seemed to anticipate the complex levels of irony and voice of Allen's humor. They also seemed ready as a generation for the topical and informed nature of his work. Even while manipulating his audience to make it laugh, Allen assumed their intelligence and awareness. At the same time, on the screen he inevitably embodied in excruciating detail the anxiety and anguish of urban claustrophobia, political and cultural alienation, and economic and environmental insecurity that students felt typified contemporary life and demanded change.

The myth of Woody Allen developed concomitantly with the growing reality of his success and fame. Indeed, the myth emerged as a complicated mixture of cinematic image, publicity, and self-serving biography. The terms *myth* and *legend* are especially appropriate for Allen because his story perpetuates precisely the kind of contradictions that true legends contain and continue. Cultivating a nebbish or schlemiel persona, he directs and works with some of the most beautiful, powerful, and sensitive women in movies and has become known for his personal relationships with many of them, including Diane Keaton and, last and probably most famously, Mia Farrow. A man of artistic genius, an individual with extraordinary power through his influence over others and his ability to control his own life, he often suggests serious, continued personal insecurities and inhibitions. With the potential to do whatever and go wherever he wants, he insists on New York as being a kind of artistic and emotional sanctuary. A student of human relationships, he remained a loner even, it seems, in his preseparation relationship with Mia Farrow, waving to her across opposing penthouse apartments overlooking New York's Central Park. Obviously needing the acclaim and attention that accompanies acting in his own films, he professes to yearn for anonymity. Although a Jew to the core, he clearly craves and achieves gentile approval. A celebrity and leading man, he relishes his ritualistic participation as an amateur clarinetist in Monday-night jazz sessions at the fashionable Michael's Pub. Appearing on the screen as a wonderfully open and caring character, off-screen it is apparently impossible to communicate directly with him unless you are Morley Safer of CBS, Maureen Dowd of the *New York Times,* or Eric Lax for the *New York*

Times Magazine. A perfectionist as a director and filmmaker, he emphasizes improvisation and instant creativity on the set. An original American auteur, he relies heavily on collaboration with great photographers like Gordon Willis and Carlo Di Palma and cowriters like Marshall Brickman. A recognized master of comedy, he has pinned his hopes for glory on the success of more serious work. Blessed in so many ways, he faces economic problems in the film industry and personal domestic difficulties that may signal a sea change in his life.

Beneath the myth and the legends of Woody Allen flows his nearly obsessive concern about his work and art. For me, this provides the key to the man and his films – how seriously he takes himself and his efforts at artistic creation. This is what we will focus on throughout this study, his work as an artist. This also remains the most controversial aspect of his career. For some, Allen suffers from seriousness and never should have departed from his sole concentration on comedy. However, what seems more important is how Allen has regarded himself and directed his own career. For 20 years, he has persistently argued that it would be easy to maintain his popularity through comedy, to do commercially successful films filled with sight gags and physical comedy – to write, act in, and direct movies that provide a platform for his verbal humor. However, as his work matured and strengthened, his ambitions and goals also changed. As he moved from stage to stage, from gag writing to performing, from screen writing and acting to complete artistic responsibility for his films, he felt increasingly compelled to deal with life and experience in totality. In attempting to fulfill the artistic, dramatic, and thematic potential of his humor and filmmaking, he tended toward developing other, complex aspects of experience. He believes that doing this requires expanding his creativity into the domains of tragedy and pathos.

In a sense, the concern for the tragic was always there as an incipient form in his earlier work. Such darkness can be discerned in how he dealt with some of his comic material. As already noted, even his previous work as a gag writer and stand-up comic, as well as elements in his early films, involved a complex, ironic, and multi dimensional perspective on subjects and material that were infused with undertones of sadness and tragedy: politics, sexuality, violence, death, chaos, failure, and alienation. Also, the frustration of formulaic work done at another's direction and the restrictions of meeting the artistic expectations of others certainly motivated him to expand his own creative horizons.

In any case, in the films dating from the early seventies through the eighties that we shall study – *Play It Again, Sam, Annie Hall, Manhattan, Zelig,*

The Purple Rose of Cairo, Hannah and Her Sisters, and *Crimes and Misdemeanors* – Allen's work takes his own comedy seriously. The characters are important even as jokes. His technical, literary, visual, and linguistic innovations are designed to introduce complexity and intensity to his humor. Instead of continuing on the proven path of zany comedy, he carefully creates films that form an original union of the serious and comedic. From the early seventies, his best work achieves a balance and integration of darkness and light.

Accordingly, I will take Allen's visual and verbal humor seriously, as part of a broader artistic achievement and innovation, partly in the hope that such a study of his depth and range ultimately will contribute to our appreciation of the humor itself. I will analyze some of his most important films of the past 20 years by describing how he puts them together and makes them work. In particular, it is necessary to examine how the humor and sadness work together and how verbal and visual humor are integrated. The films need to be viewed as a total process of complex creativity.

At the core of this process rests Allen's transition from a verbal and literary figure to a filmmaker. He becomes an artist whose genius for visual invention and creativity matches his linguistic originality until both aspects of his work cohere into an exciting art form. He learns to use shots, sequences, and visualizations with a technical dexterity and artistic creativity comparable to the use of language in his humorous writings. His films thereby become both a visual text and a literary text, an integrated cinetext of visual and verbal images and signs. This cinetextual process of creation will be examined by looking critically at individual moments within the films, by studying the films as a whole, by determining how individual shots and scenes develop depth of character and propel narration, and by relating the films to each other. It will be necessary also to consider some of the many artistic sources and influences in film and literature that Allen uses for his own cinematic creativity. As already suggested, these range widely from an extremely eclectic group of Americans, including Orson Welles and Groucho Marx, to the major European film directors from Fellini and De Sica to Bergman. Both an Englishman and an American, Charlie Chaplin is also an extraordinarily important influence in helping to shape Allen's cinematic and comedic imagination. Allen's ambition and hope, as expressed in several interviews throughout his career, to place at least some of his work in this line of great filmmaking warrants a thoughtful response.

This critical focus on Allen's work engenders a dilemma and a danger – but also an opportunity. For students of film, taking Woody Allen's somber side seriously should be considered an occupational hazard. Relating the darker aspects of his vision to the lighter glow of his humor invites charges – which I reject – of sharing his alleged pretentiousness and, even worse, of missing the point of Allen's genius at humor and his tragic flaw in moving away from a complete commitment to comedy. Such concerns about taking Allen too seriously are especially important in light of recent developments within critical theory of film and literature. To many, film and literary study have become entirely too ponderous. Applying recent theory to Allen could amount to committing a double sin of adding insult to injury by using a new critical terminology upon a comic talent that was meant for pure enjoyment. Therefore, some consideration should be given at the beginning to my methodology, to the important question of what critical and analytical tools, concepts and methods, will be used in studying his films.

In the past two decades, feminism, psychoanalysis, and semiotics have tended to dominate academic schools and approaches to film criticism. Obviously, the mere application of these critical approaches does not guarantee critical depth or power. To the contrary, their use can deaden the experience of art and film. For many, even the mention of these methods destroys the enjoyment and natural vitality of cinema and art. Nevertheless, their influence is pervasive and their use ubiquitous. It is impossible to seriously study film or literature today, especially in an academic setting, without considering feminist concerns for the place and objectification of women or without confronting psychoanalytic insights into the presence of the unconscious in hidden areas of literary and cinematic text. It also has become commonplace to use linguistic and semiotic terminology about the formation of the subject in a text as a way of discussing character, power, and meaning in a literary or cinematic work. The semiotic and linguistic use of signs and signifers within a broader signifying process that renders subjectivity and meaning appears in much contemporary criticism. Such critics also tend to give special attention to the role of art as a commodity and as part of a greater system of industrial and technological production. In combination with an appreciation for the inexorable relationship of art to the social and economic roots of culture, this body of criticism has transformed the contemporary study of literature, art, and film.

The opening chapters of this book reflect somewhat the influence of the critical thought I have described. It seems to me that Allen and much of contemporary critical theory should work well together because he concentrates so intensely on the place and situation of women, the role of psychoanalysis, and the social construction of art forms. Considering some of the insights of theory caused me to think in new ways about much of Allen's work: his use of the camera to reverse the traditional pattern of making women the object of desire in cinema; his development of narrative to dramatize desire and the working of the unconscious; his separation of the elements of cinema such as sight and sound to create interesting psychological conditions; his complex rendering of the continual fragmentation of subjectivity and identity; his visual presentation of situations of psychic, social, and linguistic alienation and separation; his self-conscious direction and cinematography that force the viewer to think about the film process itself and the viewer's own subjectivity within it.

However, for some readers, the opening chapters of this study may constitute a first exposure or introduction to aspects of current critical thinking. This is not necessarily unfortunate, considering the importance placed on such critical thought by so many writers and theorists. While wishing to engage and challenge the reader and viewer versed in current critical thought, I also would be pleased to give others an opportunity to begin thinking about how much is to be gained by working with these critical concepts and applying them to an important body of work. Obviously, any critical study such as this one needs to be questioned in terms of the case it makes for the importance and value of its subject as well as for its method of examining that subject. A study of the contribution of Woody Allen may be an agreeable and worthwhile place to start such a process and pattern of critical evaluation.

Furthermore, throughout this study, I seek to place Allen and his work within the context of American culture and history as both an artist and a creative consciousness. So isolated and different in so many ways, so anxious and intellectual, so urban and Jewish in his speech and mannerisms, Allen is also so American. The ultimate American in his awareness and representation of the world around and within him, he has become a major cultural symbol of a mind-set and way of life. The quintessential New Yorker, he is our Gatsby looking out, not at Long Island, but at the city itself with the persistent wonder and awe that, in America, all things are still possible and all transformations can and will occur.

As part of Allen's involvement in understanding and representing the American experience today, his films deal with broad social and cultural subjects, themes that comprise the core of contemporary life. Allen's intelligent treatment of these subjects contributes to the literary and intellectual aura that tends to characterize his work. The subjects that comprise the body of his work often include a self-reflexive consideration of cinema itself as an art form, the relevance of middle-class values to the complexities of modern life, the ambiguities and anxieties of Jewish identity, the joys and perils of existence in New York, the nature of comedy and its value as a form of therapy, the efficacy of psychoanalysis, and the power of love and loyalty in a corrupt society. The works suggest a genuine, if somewhat general, appreciation for and engagement with existential and ethical issues regarding human values and relationships. Allen's place in the intellectual and artistic milieu of New York City, his connection to Jewish culture and life, and his democratic and moralistic attitude toward American history and politics also make him part of a mainstream ideological perspective that frequently seems to contradict his equally strong proclivity toward nonconformity and iconoclasm.[2] Allen's films generally do not suggest an easy resolution to these tensions of modern life. Instead, he often dramatizes these issues by conveying them through a fragmented consciousness that in itself suggests psychic and social displacement. Throughout many of these films, an awareness of psychoanalysis operates as a kind of master narrative to provide some tentative means for organizing the chaos of modern experience, although for Allen even Freudian theory fails as a total solution to life's dilemmas.

Allen's work incorporates psychoanalysis and the unconscious into the very form of the films, as opposed to privileging a dominant psychoanalytical perspective, as in Alfred Hitchcock's *Marnie* and *Psycho*. Hitchcock's films usually assume a psychological voice of authority to explain character and behavior from a fairly conventional clinical point of view. In contrast, Allen tries to use visual images and language to replicate on the screen the processes of psychic instability and confusion. Allen's penchant for psychoanalysis makes his films accessible to contemporary critical approaches that focus on the place of women in cinema. These critical perspectives tend to emphasize dichotomies related to women's traditional role in classic cinema as objects or spectacles that cultivate narcissism while denying empowerment. Such critics as Stanley Cavell, Teresa de Lauretis, and Lucy Fischer maintain that these issues share a common basis in the psychoanalytic understanding of the relationship between the unconscious and cinema. For Allen, these subjects appear in his presentation of gender and sexual relationships. While some see only self-centered sexism in his work, one also can discern "sexts," a term used by Helen Cixous, the radical feminist critic, to expound the need for revealing, regarding and revolutionizing woman's body, voice, and place.[3] The result is that an Allen film often becomes a psychoanalysis of our culture and times, often one espousing major change.

While Allen's analysis in film is invariably funnier than the critics who explain it, it also is one he takes seriously. For Allen, the capacity for cinema to move fluidly between verbal script and the visual image gives the medium extraordinary power to invade individual perceptions and influence public consciousness. Vulnerable to the perverse exploitations of propaganda, cinema also can be a potent force for personal renewal and cultural regeneration, including a potential revivification of American perspectives and values. Allen's work, therefore, follows Christian Metz's notion of the "programme" of "experimental cinema" to "subvert and enrich perception, to put it in closer touch with the unconscious, to 'decensor' it as far as possible."[4]

Allen's cinematic explorations of new artistic techniques as well as broad cultural subjects parallel literary ventures into similar territory by such writers as Philip Roth and E. L. Doctorow, important American Jeremiahs who constantly attack the moral status quo. Allen puts their urbanity, ethnicity, humor, and self-deprecation into the visual dimension of film. All three assault the barriers demarcating fiction and reality, story and history, with the same audacity that characterizes their attacks on boundaries of class and prejudice. Moreover, they each experiment with the decentered narrative self to redefine authorship as a re-creative relationship between the so-called interior and exterior authors. In many of Doctorow's novels, including such recent works as *World's Fair* and *Billy Bathgate*, the internal narrators and the author exist in marriages of mutually invented identities that are as happy as Roth and his Zuckerman are destructive in their sadomasochism. Similarly, Allen, like Zelig, is inconceivable outside of the picture or photograph. In most of Allen's films, the exterior author exists in relationship to the interior narrator. For all three authors – Allen, Roth, and Doctorow – the decentered self becomes, in Kaja Silverman's term, "a synecdochic representation" of displaced consciousness and reality.[5]

While Allen's approach to and understanding of art and culture connect him to many of his contemporaries, his importance to American humor invites a comparison to an earlier literary figure as well, Mark Twain. Allen's ultimate impact on both humor in America and film as an art form ostensibly could make his achievement and place in our culture comparable to that of Twain. Whereas Twain developed frontier humor and storytelling into an original and complex art form capable of containing multiple levels of cultural and linguistic meaning, Allen has turned a gift for oral and written comedy into his personal cinematic style of integrating dialog, music, cinematography, setting, action, and characterization. Allen needed to find an artistic form that could express his humor and intellectual and personal concerns without sacrificing, as Henry Nash Smith said of Twain, "art to ideology."[6] Just as Twain learned in one tale, according to Walter Blair, to move from oral to written humor, so Allen found his vision and voice in the film version of *Play It Again, Sam* (1972), which he starred in and wrote.[7] In this film, important techniques — voice-overs, traditional frame narratives, music, and visual images — are employed in imaginative ways that are developed further in later films. He moved from simply repeating the jokes in his popular stories, comic routines, and anecdotes to the creation of original cinema. Allen dramatizes this process of self-growth from stand-up comic and gag writer to director within his own films. In *Everything You Always Wanted to Know About Sex*, we see him as a pathetic court jester. However, five years later in 1977, he documents in *Annie Hall* his own transition from disillusioned gag writer and successful stand-up comic to a serious, credible artist. As Eric Lax writes in his recent biography of Allen:

> He has grown from a comedian translating a monologue into film in *Take the Money and Run* to a character using a vast array of film techniques (split screen, cartoons, flashback, narration, stream of consciousness, fantasy) to tell his story in *Annie Hall* to an ironic commentator on values and artistic fulfillment in *Crimes and Misdemeanors*. The cinematography he has used to show his stories ranges from the crude, hand-held-camera style of *Take the Money* and *Bananas* to the deeply contrasted, Ansel Adams–like black and white in *Manhattan* to the cartoon brightness of *Radio Days* and *Alice* to the autumnal richness of *Hannah, Another Woman*, and *September*.[8]

In a pattern that continues, interestingly enough, to compare with Twain's career, Allen's humor becomes steadily more complex as he matures as an artist. In both, humor refracts hidden forces from the unconscious. Whereas Freud actually mentions Twain in *Civilization and Its Discontents* as an example of the psychoanalytic uses of humor, Allen is like Roth in his self-conscious exploitation of Freud to intensify the effect of voicing the unspeakable.[9] While Allen joins Twain, Roth, and so many others in using humor as a force for destruction and reconstruction, he also advances a modern technology of humor through his use of the camera, screenwriting, and direction in his films. In the canon of Allen's major films, *Play It Again, Sam* is, as already noted, a transitional work. As Nancy Pogel notes, "In this early Allen film, there are foreshadowings of the later films where filmmaker, audience, and characters will all be implicated more seriously in a modern viewpoint that permits no comforting certainties about what constitutes fiction." Thus, *Play It Again, Sam* initiates a process of artistic development through *Annie Hall, Manhattan, Broadway Danny Rose, The*

Purple Rose of Cairo, *Hannah and Her Sisters*, and *Crimes and Misde-meanors*. These works demonstrate an artistic progression in which cine-matic creativity reinforces an ideology of social and cultural reconstruction and revision. Submitting these films to what William Rothman calls "a reading of the sequence, moment by moment" will reveal Allen's rediscovery of basic questions of sexuality, social identity and consciousness, existence, and morality.[10]

The fact that not Woody Allen but Herb Ross actually directed *Play It Again, Sam* helps to mark the film as a transitional work for Allen. Ross worked from Allen's screenplay, an adaptation from Allen's successful Broadway play. Before *Play It Again, Sam*, Allen directed and wrote *Take the Money and Run* and *Bananas*. The separation for Allen of the tasks of writing and directing in *Play It Again, Sam* signifies a moment of anticipation and preparation for the artistic fulfillment of his subsequent films. Not quite ready for the leap to being both director and writer in this major innovative work, Allen's acceptance of the division of labor in this film emphasizes the transition in his creative career from so-called zany and idiosyncratic pop-ular comedy to films of heightened sensitivity and moral complexity. The gap between the roles of director and writer suggests a pause before achiev-ing the artistic maturity that now characterizes Allen's work. Obviously, the credit for the professionalism and talent of the direction belongs to Ross. However, Allen's creative imagination as articulated and presented in the screenplay clearly dominate the film and place it within the Allen canon. The humor, energy, manipulation of reality and fantasy, unconventional narrative technique, characterization, and plotting bear Allen's distinctive signature and contrast dramatically with Ross's most successful films since *Play It Again, Sam*, such as *The Turning Point*, *The Seven Per Cent Solution*, and *The Goodbye Girl*.

From the moment that *Play It Again, Sam* first appears on the screen, we realize that we are viewing a different kind of film. *Play It Again, Sam* opens with its movie critic hero, Allan Felix, entranced as he views *Casablanca* in a New York theater. More than just another movie about movies, the film's opening, as we soon will see, relates the complex analogies between the formation of both the subject in language and the spectator in cinema to the construction of gender in society. It connects the unconscious ambiguities of sexual organization and gender construction to the social process of investing meaning in the signs and signifiers of sexual difference, subjectivity, and social identity. In other words, it relates the process of achieving sexual identity and subjectivity to the processes of signs and language that define and develop such identity and subjectivity. Allen's enactment of the signifying process – the relationship of signs and signifiers to the things and objects that are named and signified – and his entrapment and construction of the viewer within it demonstrates the dependence of subjectivity and identity upon visual and other signs or signifiers of experience. In the beginning moments of this movie, we get visible confirmation, as Silverman says, "of the subject as a complex of signifying processes."[1] In effect, we witness the semiotic invention of identity and reality. As the film progresses, it also will confirm what this scene powerfully suggests about the sexual rootedness of the relationship between subjectivity and the social construction of gender.

Important to this issue of subjectivity and signification in *Play It Again, Sam* is the fact that, in an Allen film, we usually begin with a split self that dramatizes the continuous construction of the subject. The camera and sound in the opening scene of the film demonstrate this process; but before discussing them, we should note that division and construction receive help from a crucial split in all of Woody Allen's films in which he appears. This involves the division between Woody Allen, the public personality, writer, and star, and the character he plays – in this case, Allan Felix. Allen exploits this division to control the audience's expectations of him as a humorist. Just his appearance on the screen will provoke laughter. In *Play It Again, Sam*, even the similarity of names becomes a joke. Allen manipulates that expectation of humor into a complex art. He uses the distinction between himself as interior character and external personality and director to introduce psychological, thematic, and artistic complexity into his subjects, characterizations, and narratives.

The opening shots of *Play It Again, Sam* demonstrate and repeat a process of shifting and volatile subjectivity for both the viewer and Allan Felix. As Allan watches *Casablanca* on the screen, subjectivity and identity become largely ephemeral. Felix floats from being the imaginary subject of the action of the movie to being simply a viewer who loses his identity and ability to act through his total immersion into the interior film *Casablanca,* which, to some extent, becomes the subject of the film *Play It Again, Sam*. Ross's camera, of course, conveys the images of changing subjectivity, but the artistic and moral vision of a democratic fluidity between subjects and viewers remains Allen's. The sequence of shots from Bergman and Bogart to Allen and back again demonstrates the fragmented and disjointed nature of subjectivity. The visual images duplicate and dramatize psychic division. This interlacing of glances and shots involving Bergman, Bogart, and Felix places Felix psychologically in the film *Casablanca*. Bergman's gaze from the screen to Felix constitutes a life-giving act, endowing him with a new identity and reality in the darkened theater.

In *Play It Again, Sam*, the presentation of divided subjectivity through the original use of camera and sound infuses psychic division and separation into the very form, structure, and substance of the film. In the opening scenes of the film, sound and image often are dramatically separated. Through most of this sequence, when we hear *Casablanca* we are looking at Allan Felix, and when we look at *Casablanca* there is little that is said. Indeed, when some of the most important lines are spoken, we see them anticipated on Allan Felix's face. This careful separation of sight and sound creates an interesting psychological effect, by reinforcing the split subject of Woody Allen's interior and exterior selves, suggesting a division within the signifying process itself as visual and auditory signs break from what seem to be signified. Words, visual images, sounds do not signify or cohere according to usual expectations. Language and visual images suggest new meanings, often with a humorous undercurrent. Again, the instance of Bergman's apparent glance, not at Bogart, but at Felix in the audience, exemplifies this cinetextual transformation of the signifying process. Moreover, the separation of sight and sound takes us away from the movie on the interior screen, *Casablanca,* and positions us to enter into Felix's divided consciousness as we not only hear and see through him, but participate in his reactions.

This split subject comprises a cinetextual counterpart to what Julia Kristeva discusses as the condition of *chora,* a semiotic process describing the situation that precedes the syntactical organization and coherence of the paternal, symbolic period in psychological development. Kristeva writes:

> Plato's *Timeus* speaks of a *chora* ... receptacle ... unnamable, improbable, hybrid, anterior to naming, to the One, to the father, and consequently, maternally connoted to such an extent that it merits "not even the rank of syllable." One can describe more precisely than did philosophical intuition the particularities of this signifying disposition that I have just named semiotic – a term which quite clearly designates that we are dealing with a disposition that is definitely heterogeneous to meaning but always in sight of it or in either a negative or surplus relationship to it.[12]

Lacanian feminist critics such as Juliet Mitchell, Jacqueline Rose, and Jane Gallop discuss this situation as the pre-Oedipal, prelinguistic stage of images that precedes symbolic order and meaning and the Oedipal break into language. Rigid perimeters between fantasy and reality, interior psychological space and external reality, unfulfilled desire and moral prohibition become blurred.

This stage, which is a semiotic, presymbolic phase of development, describes the condition in which we find Allan Felix in the beginning of *Play It Again, Sam*. The darkened theater becomes a linguistic womb, a fresh beginning for Felix that disrupts ordinary organization and development. Most important, the split psyche and subject imply a disordering of conventional sexual organization that creates the possibility for new sexual ordering. Indeed, Allan Felix's condition and place before the screen in the theater suggest the kind of passivity that once was assumed to be part of feminine nature. Allan Felix takes what Stanley Cavell calls "the position of the feminine" in that he shares with women the classic Hollywood camera's proclivity toward their objectification and "victimization."[13] From Felix's infantile perspective in the theater, Bergman and Bogart are the classic fantasy parents of the Freudian "family romance" in which the child invents parents that confirm his or her secret wish for sexual, emotional, and physical omnipotence.[14] Felix clearly loves both Bogart and Bergman and wants to be loved by and to possess both. Thus, the complex opening scenes of separated shots and sounds use the visual and auditory signs of cinema to suggest the sexual ambivalence and insecurity that haunt Allan Felix. The film not only tells us about this situation and gives us a character who embodies it, it renders the condition of sexual uncertainty in the form of the reorganization of the movie's signifying process. The reordering of language and image in this scene replicates Felix's internal disorder and anticipates his search for love and identity.

Reliving the moments of *Casablanca* on some deep psychic level, Allan Felix's facial contortions while viewing it render a seismic record of everything he sees and hears on the screen. Not surprisingly, when *Casablanca* ends and the lights go on, Allan Felix finds himself as confused as someone waking from a dream, suddenly uncertain of his identity and distressed by his surroundings. For Allan Felix, the world on the screen seems especially real and intimate when compared with his daily existence. His depression on leaving the theater and the domination of his bedroom by Bogart posters further suggest his fragile psychic state. In the universe of signifying relationships, cinema and theater and on- and off-screen reality exist and operate on a continuum of experience.

Incorporating, as we said, the unconscious and semiotic within its very form, *Play It Again, Sam* emphasizes the materiality of film by bringing attention to the various elements of camera shot and sound track that comprise film. In addition, the film also makes the important connection between the structure and nature of films and the way dreams are formed and function. As Silverman says, "Because one of the registers of its inscription is that used by the unconscious in the production of dreams," film "has the capacity not only to depict the displacements of waking desire but to do so in a language familiar to the sleeping subject." The characteristics of dreams that originally inspired Freud in *The Interpretation of Dreams* to say, "*the interpretation of dream is the royal road to a knowledge of the unconscious activities of the mind,*" are intrinsic to Allen's major films – symbolism, disordered narrative and time sequence, the separation of the senses, the condensation of complex, often contradictory, meanings and events into imaginary or distorted images, the displacement of latent, inner realities by invented experiences that seem ludicrous or incredible until analyzed.[15] Obviously, these same aspects of dreams lend themselves to humorous uses, as Freud himself maintained in *Jokes and Their Relation to the Unconscious*. Of course, the use of these elements of dreams has become a trademark of Allen's films. *Casablanca* becomes Allan Felix's dream, endlessly repeated because it structures in a symbolic form his innermost yearnings, fears, and aggressions. Felix's compulsion to repeat the experience of the movie is at once pathetic, neurotic, and humorous.

Moreover, Allan Felix's experience in the theater seems to be an almost perfect dramatization of Jean-Louis Baudry's poststructuralist theory of the psychoanalytic dimension of cinema. Baudry says that "taking into account the darkness of the movie theater, the relative passivity of the situation, the forced immobility of the cine-subject, and the effects which result from the projection of images, moving images, the cinematographic apparatus brings about a state of artificial regression." Remembering that Felix undergoes precisely this kind of regression in a setting similar to Baudry's description of the cinematic situation, Baudry's formulation of the relationship between cinema and the unconscious mind of the viewer helps to explain the process behind Felix's psychic state as he views *Casablanca*. Baudry goes on to say of cinema's effect on the viewer:

It artificially leads back to an anterior phase of his development – a phase which is barely hidden, as dream and certain pathological forms of our mental life have shown. It is the desire, unrecognized as such by the subject, to return to this phase, an early state of development with its own forms of satisfaction which may play a determining role in his desire for cinema and the pleasure he finds in it. Return toward a relative narcissism, and even more toward a mode of relating to reality which could be defined as enveloping and in which the separation between one's own body and the exterior world is not well defined. Following this line of reasoning, one may then be able to understand the reasons for the intensity of the subject's attachment to the images and the process of identification created by cinema. A return to a primitive narcissism by the regression of the libido, Freud tells us, noting that the dreamer occupies the entire field of the dream scene; the absence of delimitation of the body; the transfusion of the interior out into the exterior . . . without excluding other processes of identification which derive from the specular regime of the ego, from its constitution as "Imaginary."[16]

The relevance of Baudry's contemporary psychoanalytical and semiological theory to *Play It Again, Sam* suggests something of the complexity and originality of Allen's understanding of film.

In the years since *Play It Again, Sam* first appeared, repeated showings of the film have made it part of our popular consciousness so those famous classic scenes from *Casablanca* seem like the inevitable beginning of the film. In fact, we remember that the original play on Broadway actually opened with Felix watching Bogart in *The Maltese Falcon* tell Mary Astor that she would have to take the fall for her crimes in spite of – or perhaps secretly because of – his love for her. There are some important benefits from this change that reflect the transition from Allen's play to the film. In the movie version, *Play It Again, Sam* plays scenes from *Casablanca* in which Bogart speaks two of *Casablanca*'s most famous and important lines that could serve as epigraphs to frame and introduce the Allen movie. "We'll always have Paris" – a line repeated sardonically later in *Manhattan* – and "Here's looking at you, kid."

In other words, absence and presence. The lines from *Casablanca* can be interpreted to typify the central concerns of film in general, according to Cavell, and of *Play It Again, Sam* in particular, as well as all of Allen's films since. To psychoanalytically oriented critics such as Cavell, Silverman, and Metz, cinematic images rest upon absence. To them, cinema's dependence upon image, as opposed to the physical presence of characters or text as in drama and reading, influences the viewer's response and the cinematic experience. The idea that "the film is the medium of visible absence," as Cavell says, suggests how film epitomizes the psychoanalytical condition and situation of what has come to be called desire or the inability to achieve ultimate sexual or emotional fulfillment and identity because of the split and fragmented nature of the human psyche.[17] In this sense, absence, presence, and desire are at the heart of Allen's interest and work. In his work since *Play It Again, Sam,* visual appearances are signs of displacement and separation, of unbridgeable gaps between unfathomable experience and inadequate symbols of frustration, of the unspeakable unconscious and the conscious search for meaning. For Allen, visual signs are masks for buried experiences that grow more and more distant the more one tries to chase them down.

Equally significant in the replacement of *The Maltese Falcon* by *Casablanca* in the film version of *Play It Again, Sam* is the resulting change from Sam Spade, the nearly pathological hero of the Dashiell Hammett story, to Rick of *Casablanca.* It is not just that Rick is a far more sympathetic character than Sam Spade. Rick is the classic American hero altered by the movement from the Western frontier to the frontier of the impending battle against fascism. To make this point it should not be necessary to review the entire film, but only to reiterate what has been said about it over the years by so many critics and audiences. Reluctant, stoic, isolated, and charismatic, Rick is the embodiment of the archetypal American hero of classic and popular culture. He epitomizes the external hardness and indifference that masks the inner yearnings and earnestness of the American hero. By using this Bogart character as a vehicle for further fragmentation and decentering of subjectivity, Allen explores the relationship of cinematic text to cultural and social text. The screenplay and images of *Play It Again, Sam* overlap with the cultural codes of American heroism, manhood, and commitment. Indeed, the association and development of the Bogart figure in *Play It Again, Sam* would be meaningless if it did not take place within a broader field of significance that has deep historic roots in our culture. By integrating the Bogart code and hero within the process of cinematic reconsideration, Allen establishes a means for proffering the reconstruction of American character. He contrives a new American hero that is similar to the new hero of thought and sensitivity in the work of Roth, Doctorow, and Bellow. From the midst of psychic fragmentation and visual displacement there emerges a vulnerable hero with an intense interior life who articulates his fears and exposes his emotional dependence on others – and makes us laugh to boot. In contrast to the classic Bogart myth of American manhood, Allen's hero finds love and identity by revealing rather than repressing pain, fear, and dependence. For the Allen hero, emotional expression means empowerment through parody, sarcasm, and humor. Such humor contaminates the privileged detachment of the Bogart hero and vitiates his hard-boiled isolationism and his immunity from commitment and dependence.

18

Allen conveys the psychology and character of this new American hero through a series of extremely humorous scenes and moments. Felix's fantasy of physical violence and booze-inspired seduction shatters into a squeaky yes when the doorbell rings. Every action and pretense of stereotypical masculine power portrays its opposite: lack of stature, impotence, fear, and even deceit and betrayal as opposed to inner strength and loyalty. The humor in these scenes gains added emotional impact through its suggestion of subsurface tension, complexity, and uncertainty. His battles with a hair dryer and various powders, deodorants, and cosmetics; his dependence upon aspirin, Darvon, and other drugs; and his failures at social conversation and casual dating all certify him as an anxious nebbish. They also suggest a deep-seated sexual uncertainty and inadequacy that extends from him to the culture as a whole as evidenced by other elements in the film, including the relationship between Diane Keaton and Tony Roberts, the characterizations of other female figures, and the implied criticism of contemporary life-styles.

A neglected dimension of Allen's work involves this subversion, as seen in *Play It Again, Sam,* of sexual stereotypes, gender roles, and cultural archetypes. Because of the profound changes inspired during the past 20 years by both the sexual and the women's revolutions, it is easy to disregard the place of *Play It Again, Sam* in this continuing social, cultural, and sexual transformation. The film's impulse for change perhaps seems muted when compared to the efforts of movements for drastic sexual and gender reform. In fact, instead of being recognized for engaging these controversial issues and moving toward change, Allen, like Philip Roth, often has been misinterpreted and vilified for his treatment of sex and gender.

Such criticism of both Allen and Roth seems misplaced. In retrospect, Allen in *Play It Again, Sam* could echo Roth's claim to be one of the first on the beachhead of the sexual revolution.[18] Moreover, the grounding of Allen's work in psychoanalysis and semiotics means that such reconsideration of sexuality, gender, and character occurs from the ground up, so to speak, from the psychological to the cultural. Sharing an appreciation for Freud with Roth, Allen's insights into sexuality, gender, and culture stand on a theory of the unconscious and sexual difference as well as ideology. *Play It Again, Sam,* therefore, encourages the Freudian impulse toward the recognition of and encounter with the other or opposite gender that comprises an aspect of one's self and character.

Further explanation of Freud's theory on this subject might be helpful in suggesting the depth of Allen's own appreciation for the complexity of these issues of sexuality and gender. As Freud developed his initial theories of sexuality, he placed increasing emphasis on sexual ambivalence and the overall uncertainty of sexual designations and characteristics ascribed to masculinity and femininity. In 1915 he added an important footnote to *Three Essays on the Theory of Sexuality* in which he asserted "that the concepts of 'masculine' and 'feminine', whose meaning seems so unambiguous to ordinary people, are among the most confused that occur in science." Freud distinguished between three uses of these terms, the sociological, which derives from observation of social behavior, the biological, which concerns physical attributes, and the most important, "the sense of activity and passivity." He writes:

> Such observation shows that in human beings pure masculinity or femininity is not to be found either in a psychological or biological sense. Every individual on the contrary displays a mixture of the character-traits belonging to his own and to the opposite sex; and he shows a combination of activity and passivity whether or not these last character-traits tally with his biological ones.[19]

Freud pursued this insight into sexual uncertainty and ambivalence. Assuming that the theory itself continued to require much greater investigation and study, he articulated and clarified it as his theory of bisexuality. In *Civilization and Its Discontents,* he writes:

> The theory of bisexuality is still surrounded by many obscurities and we cannot but feel it as a serious impediment in psychoanalysis that it has not yet found any link with the theory of the instincts. However this may be, if we assume it as a fact that each individual seeks to satisfy both male and female wishes in his sexual life, we are prepared for the possibility that those [two sets of] demands are not fulfilled by the same object, and that they interfere with each other unless they can be kept apart and each impulse guided into a particular channel that is suited to it.[20]

After further reflection upon the complexity of this issue of bisexuality, near the end of his life and career Freud came to see this sexual ambivalence as a special source of conflict and pathology. Both men and women were continually in contention with the opposite sex within themselves. Evidencing a degree of his own Victorian sexism and latent ambiguity toward women, Freud maintained in "Analysis Terminable and Interminable" (1937) that, in women, sexual ambivalence often led to certain forms of overaggression, while in men it inspired a crippling fear of castration and dependence.[21]

It can be argued that one of the most interesting and powerful aspects of *Play It Again, Sam* concerns how Woody Allen and Diane Keaton, as the characters Allan Felix and Linda Christie, develop a relationship that responds to the kind of sexual ambivalence Freud describes. They are sexual counterparts. Linda cultivates and brings out the feminine in Felix's character, while Felix proffers the love Linda lacks and encourages her to move beyond passivity and become more aggressive in articulating her emotional and personal needs as a woman and wife. Beneath the awkwardness and insecurity of their initial lovemaking rests the more basic uncertainty of sexuality and gender roles and definitions. Felix overcompensates for the feminine part of his nature by fantasizing about ridiculous notions of exaggerated masculine sexual prowess in the form of the Bogart hero. Linda, on the other hand, failing to deal with her husband's neglect, internalizes her anger and frustration by developing a deep sense of inadequacy, insecurity, and guilt. Expressing the feminine side of his nature makes Felix a man to and with her, while also inspiring her to act and develop a voice and persona of her own.

Felix's unconscious ambivalence achieves humorous but definite expression in a crucial parapraxis or misstatement that, according to Freud, reveals latent or repressed wishes and fears. It occurs while Linda and Felix are at a discotheque. Felix is wildly attracted to a young girl on the dance floor (Fig. 1). Significantly, Felix links his feelings toward her with a comment about his mother: "She's a doll! I would sell my mother to the Arabs for that girl!" As Linda urges him to dance with her, Felix says, "I love you, Miss – whoever you are – I want to have your child." Of course, the statement could easily be dismissed as the product of nervous overstimulation; but, in fact, it advances what could be called the "feminine" side of his nature – to be possessed, to bear life, and to nurture – which has been present throughout the film. Instead of perpetuating sexist attitudes, this scene, as a miniature of the entire film, undermines conventional attitudes. Visually the scene says one thing: Felix once again agonizes over a beautiful woman. The language, however, subverts that sexual intention, revealing disguised desires, while his relationship with Linda contradicts the Bogart ideology of insensitive male aggressiveness. Thus, the cinetext also delineates a counterideology of love and vulnerability that the unconscious both requires and represses.

In *Play It Again, Sam*, love, as Freud would have it, does not solve the problems of human relationships or absolve one of guilt for committing wrong; but it does help one to mature. Love enables Felix to escape the endless repetition of his "family romance" and to overcome his obsession

Figure 1. Woody Allen, as Allan Felix in *Play It Again, Sam,* tries to pick up a dancer, played by Suzanne Zenor, at a disco. (Courtesy of Paramount Pictures. *Play It Again, Sam,* copyright © 1972 by Paramount Pictures; all rights reserved.)

with Bogart in order to become his own man. As Felix says, "I'm short enough and ugly enough to succeed by myself." Learning to live with himself rather than by imitating false models, Felix really confronts aspects of his character that are hidden, but frightening sources of strength. Similarly, Linda makes a mature decision to return to her husband, Dick, using language that can be interpreted as blatantly suggestive of Freud's insights into sexuality.

Moreover, Felix and Linda also fulfill Freud's prophecy that, as individuals, all we can ever achieve is the transformation of "hysterical misery into common unhappiness."[22] And yet great social, cultural, and artistic changes have occurred. A reconstruction of character and experience has transpired before our eyes. Both the interior and exterior narrators of *Play It Again, Sam* have been transformed. Felix declares his readiness to stand alone, while Woody Allen emerges as a figure of major importance. Felix walks off into the fog to find his destiny (in the play version this takes the form of a new girl). Woody, in turn, goes off to achieve new levels of acclaim and recognition in *Annie Hall*. Abandoning Bogart becomes more than a personal triumph, but a cultural transition as well.

Notes

1. See Douglas Brode, *Woody Allen: His Films and Career*, 2nd ed. (Secaucus, N.J.: Citadel, 1987), p. 13.

2. See Sam B. Girgus, *The New Covenant: Jewish Writers and the American Idea* (Chapel Hill: University of North Carolina Press, 1984) for a discussion of this theme in terms of a tradition of Jewish writers and thinkers who identify with and speak for American culture, while at the same time criticizing moral and political failures.

3. See Helene Cixous and Catherine Clement, "Sorties: Out and Out: Attacks/ Ways Out/Forays" and "Exchange" in *The Newly Born Woman*, trans. Betsy Wing (Minneapolis: University of Minnesota Press, 1986), pp. 63–260.

4. Christian Metz, *The Imaginary Signifier: Psychoanalysis and the Cinema*, trans. Celia Britton, Annwyl Williams, Ben Brewster, and Alfred Guzzetti (Bloomington: Indiana University Press, 1982), pp. 289–90.

5. Kaja Silverman, *The Acoustic Mirror: The Female Voice in Psychoanalysis and Cinema* (Bloomington: Indiana University Press, 1988), p. 31.

6. Henry Nash Smith, *Mark Twain: The Development of a Writer* (New York: Atheneum, 1967), p. 137.

7. Walter Blair and Hamlin Hill, *America's Humor: From Poor Richard to Doonesbury* (New York: Oxford University Press, 1978), pp. 333–48.

8. Eric Lax, *Woody Allen: A Biography* (New York: Knopf, 1991), p. 274.

9. Sigmund Freud, *Civilization and Its Discontents*, trans. James Strachey (New York: Norton, 1972), p. 73, n. 2

10. Nancy Pogel, *Woody Allen* (Boston: Twayne, 1987), p. 48; William Rothman, *The "I" of the Camera: Essays in Film Criticism, History, and Aesthetics* (Cambridge University Press, 1988), p. xii.

11. Kaja Silverman, *The Subject of Semiotics* (New York: Oxford University Press, 1983), p. 148.

12. Julia Kristeva, *Desire in Language: A Semiotic Approach to Literature and Art*,

ed. Leon S. Roudiez, trans. Thomas Gora, Alice Jardine, and Leon S. Roudiez (New York: Columbia University Press, 1980), p. 133.

13. Stanley Cavell, "The Melodrama of the Unknown Woman," in *Images in Our Souls: Cavell, Psychoanalysis, and Cinema,* ed. Joseph H. Smith and William Kerrigan (Baltimore: Johns Hopkins University Press, 1987), pp. 11–43; rpt. in *The Trial(s) of Psychoanalysis,* ed. Francoise Meltzer (Chicago: University of Chicago Press, 1988), p. 256.

14. Sigmund Freud, "Family Romance," *Standard Edition of the Complete Psychological Works* (London: Hogarth, 1959), 9:235.

15. Silverman, *The Subject of Semiotics,* p. 85; Freud, *The Interpretation of Dreams* (1900; rpt. New York: Avon Discus, 1965), p. 647.

16. Jean-Louis Baudry, "The Apparatus: Metapsychological Approaches to the Impression of Reality in the Cinema" in *Film Theory and Criticism: Introductory Readings,* eds. Gerald Mast, Marshall Cohen, Lee Braudy, 4th ed. (New York: Oxford University Press, 1992), pp. 703–4.

17. Stanley Cavell here renders a visual version of Freud's famous caveat in "The Most Prevalent Form of Degradation in Erotic Life" (1912) that "we must reckon with the possibility that something in the nature of the sexual instinct itself is unfavourable to the realisation of complete satisfaction." See Cavell, "The Melodrama of the Unknown Woman," p. 255. See also Freud, *Standard Edition of the Complete Psychological Works* 11:188–9, rpt. in *Freud: Sexuality and the Psychology of Love,* ed. Philip Rieff (New York: Collier, 1963), p. 68. Similarly, Juliet Mitchell says, "Desire persists as an effect of a primordial absence and it therefore indicates, that in this area, there is something fundamentally impossible about satisfaction itself." See Mitchell, "Introduction-I," *Feminine Sexuality: Jacques Lacan and the ecole freudienne,* eds. Juliet Mitchell and Jacqueline Rose (New York: Norton, 1982), p. 6. For a more detailed discussion of the theory of desire, see also Sam Girgus, *Desire and the Political Unconscious in American Literature* (New York: Macmillan and St. Martin's Press, 1990).

18. Philip Roth, *Reading Myself and Others* (New York: Farrar, Straus & Giroux, 1975), p. 8.

19. Sigmund Freud, *Three Essays on the Theory of Sexuality,* trans. James Strachey, intro. Steven Marcus (1905; rpt. New York: Harper Colophon Basic Books, 1975), pp. 85–6, n. 1.

20. Freud, *Civilization and Its Discontents,* p. 53, n. 3.

21. Sigmund Freud, "Analysis Terminable and Interminable" in *The Standard Edition of the Complete Psychological Works,* 23:252, writes: "At no other point in analytic work does one suffer more from an oppressive feeling that all one's repeated efforts have been in vain, and from a suspicion that one has been 'preaching to the winds', than when one is trying to persuade a woman to abandon her wish for a penis on the ground of its being unrealizable or when one is seeking to convince a man that a passive attitude to men does not always signify castration and that it is indispensable in many relationships in life. The rebellious overcompensation of the male produces one of the strongest transferences-resistances."

22. Josef Breuer and Sigmund Freud, *Studies in Hysteria* in *The Standard Edition of the Complete Psychological Works,* 2:305.

2

Desire and
Narrativity in
Annie Hall

"At the origin of Narrative, desire," writes Roland Barthes, saving his for the end of the sentence.[1] Partly because of Barthes's influence, this theory of the fusion of desire and narrativity has become central for many critics and students of literature and cinema, especially those who tend to emphasize the connection between semiotics and psychoanalysis. According to this theory, narrativity, as the organization of the processes of sign production and subjectivity in cinema, originates in the Oedipal experience of sexual difference. Desire – the establishment of sexual differences through the displacement of the unconscious upon language and symbols – finds itself in narrative.[2] Desire and narrative function together as two ineluctable parts of the same process of the unending search for self and identity. All narrative emerges out of this basic, most personal of stories involving the interaction between unconscious forces and culture. Thus, Teresa de Lauretis sees "desire as a function of narrative and narrativity as a process engaging that desire." She writes, "The work of narrative, then, is a mapping of differences, and specifically, first and foremost, of sexual difference into each text."[3]

In this formulation, desire, narrativity, and Oedipus operate interdependently and intertextually, thereby effecting an important movement of post-Freudian critical theory from drives and ego relations to language and signs. Oedipus provides the basis for character development, while the Freudian narrative of repression and return enables us to talk about the unspeakable and to see in disguised form the desire that remains hidden from personal consciousness and the moral imagination. The relationship of narrative and desire to feminine and masculine gender construction remains a basic concern in feminist and psychoanalytical theories of cinema. Both men and women are formed in this relationship between desire and narrative. As de Lauretis says:

While Oedipus is he who answers the riddle posed by the Sphinx, Freud stands in both places at once, for he first formulates – defines – the question and then answers it. And we shall see that his question, what is femininity, acts precisely as the impulse, the desire that will generate a narrative, the story of femininity, or how a (female) child with a bisexual disposition becomes a little girl and then a woman.[4]

The special relationship between desire and narrative, as described by de Lauretis, in which desire operates as a function of narrativity and narrativity in turn processes desire, can be found in *Annie Hall* (1977), which Allen coauthored with Marshall Brickman. In the first place, the opening speech by Alvy Singer and the scenes that follow it exemplify the complex nature of narrativity in contemporary discourse. We move from Alvy Singer's direct address to the audience to a sequence of scenes that thrusts a radical dislocation of chronological order on us. Such chronological dislocation characterizes the entire film's treatment of time and space. Thus, in these first scenes we go directly from Alvy's address to a visit during his childhood to the family doctor, to his childhood home allegedly under a Coney Island roller coaster, to a boardwalk scene, to a bumper-car concession, to his schoolroom and brief biographies of his classmates in which the children announce what will happen to them in the future, to a TV screen that shows Alvy "as an adult on a talk show" with Dick Cavett, back to Alvy's house as a youth, and then to a scene from the assumed present with Alvy and his best friend Rob, played by Tony Roberts, walking on a Manhattan street.[5] Significantly, in this last scene we hear Alvy's and Rob's voices but do not immediately see them because they are walking toward the camera from a distance on the street that is beyond the camera's range. This promiscuous use of time and space in *Annie Hall* drastically alters the ordinary order of events and the traditional spatial connection of happenings of conventional story format and structure. The pattern of dislocation – or the absence of a rigid pattern – exemplifies the distinction contemporary critics make between *histoire* – the order of events to which a story refers – and narrative discourse – the events presented in the discourse as organized by plot.[6]

Moreover, Alvy's narration dramatizes a crucial point that Peter Brooks makes about the relationship between *histoire* and narrative discourse.[7] The events of the *histoire* – or *diegesis* – seem to have most importance because they supposedly really occurred. They therefore have priority over and make possible those events that go into the plot or discourse – *mimesis*. However, the events of the *histoire* actually are themselves "a mental construction" that the reader or, in the case of a film such as *Annie Hall,* the viewer in a significantly different way learns through discourse or mimesis. In other words, what really happened or what we really see comes to us as narrative. The real events of *histoire* are dependent on the ability to put those events into narrative discourse. As Brooks states, this connection between *histoire* and narrative "by no means invalidates the distinction itself, which is central to our thinking about narrative and necessary to its analysis since it allows us to juxtapose two modes of order and in the juxtaposing to see how ordering takes place."[8] In Alvy's case, the seemingly chaotic temporal and spatial activities of the narrative underscore the uncertainty of the diegesis, or what supposedly really happened, including growing up under a roller coaster. Allen therefore demonstrates the important relationship between these two aspects or modes of narrative. *Annie Hall* so startled and delighted audiences when it first appeared partly because of Allen's exciting manipulation of this inherent tension between diegesis and mimesis. This narrative tension in the film also proffers something of an artistic declaration of the work's independence and importance. It insists upon a denial of artistic and creative closure and further demands the kind of continual analysis and reinterpretation expected of serious cinema and art.

Allen also explores the dichotomy between diegesis and mimesis in *The Purple Rose of Cairo* (1985) in which a lonely woman named Cecilia returns so often to a local theater to watch a movie that the film's main character steps out of the screen to get to know her. Their subsequent romance and comic adventure collapse the boundary between fantasy and reality and constitute an important statement about the power of mass media over the individual and public. However, the situation of the movie also dramatizes the distinction between narrative discourse and *histoire* in terms, for Cecilia, of fantasy and fiction, and these terms come to dominate her understanding of the world. For Cecilia, intertextuality is not a complex theory of reading and interpretation, but a way of life. The combination of fantasy and self-referential textuality in Cecilia's narrative makes her experience comparable to the world of dreams.

Dreams, Freud would seem to suggest, dramatically relax the differences between *histoire* and narrative discourse through their apparent emphasis on fiction and illusion as a means for perceiving reality. Through the interpretation of what Freud called the "dream text" and the analysis of the analysand, one constructs an understanding of the events that theoretically helped the formation of the dream. We work through the narrative of the dream, which is already part of a process of "secondary revision," to relate the manifest material of the dream to an individual's sense of reality. In

Freudian interpretations, dreams are by definition dislocated and disordered psychic events that relate to experiences that are in turn also dislocated and disordered in the unconscious. No natural order of events obtains for dream narratives. Time, history, and space also are severely fractured in their relationship to the unconscious and the formation of the dream. Thus, it would appear that the natural tendency of *histoire* toward creating the illusion of reality, which it really derives from narrative, seems somewhat abated. To paraphrase Barthes, in dreams the code of interpretation or enigma seems to dominate the code of action.

Dreams not only emphasize the importance of narrative discourse and interpretation, they also dramatize the centrality of desire to narrative. For Freud, of course, sexuality and desire are key to the formation of dreams. Similarly, desire drives events into narrative structure. Desire facilitates the interaction between *histoire* and narrative and between action and interpretation. Desire puts the body and the unconscious into our organization of events. Defining "inherently unsatisfied and unsatisfiable" desire "as a perpetual want for (of) satisfaction that cannot be offered in reality," Brooks maintains desire's ineluctable connection to narrative. All reading, he says, is a form of desire that becomes a " 'textual erotics.' "[9] Narrative embodies and structures desire in the force of desire's drive toward completion or an end. While events intensely strive toward organization through narrative, narrative in turn yearns for the meaning of an ending:

> The desire of the text (the desire of reading) is hence desire for the end, but desire for the end reached only through the at least minimally complicated detour, the intentional deviance, in tension which is the plot of narrative.... The desire of the text is ultimately the desire for the end, for that recognition which is the moment of the death of the reader in the text.[10]

Moreover, just as *histoire* entails a working out of events through narrative, so also all narrative constitutes an *"anticipation of retrospection."* "The nature of narration" to be "a repetitive recapitulative mechanism" compels narrative to use desire as its vehicle for failed completion and impossible fulfillment.[11] Accordingly, all narrative involves at least some degree of a journey through unconscious desire in an attempt to revisit and reinterpret the origins of narrative desire. "Retrospective desire satisfies itself in the recall and recounting of unobtainable objects."[12]

The theory of the complex relationship of desire, narrative, and language achieves wonderful simplicity and clarity in the visual and verbal humor of Allen's *Annie Hall.* The inherent desire of narrative for an ending manifests itself about two-thirds of the way into Alvy Singer's opening monologue. "Annie and I broke up and I – I still can't get my mind around that" (p. 4). Thus, Alvy gives us the ending of the story before he really gets started into the process of telling it. The "anticipation of retrospection" becomes clear in the attempt through repetition to understand the significance of this failed love relationship. The eruption of this thought about Annie from the midst of so much seemingly irrelevant material dramatizes the existence of latent desires and replicates in the text the tension of the unconscious in Alvy. Significantly, the subject of the outburst involves desire – for Annie. In the spirit of desire and psychoanalysis, the narrative goes forward by going backward over Alvy's past and his personal history of desire. He takes us through his childhood to one of his first kisses and one of his first encounters with rejection by the opposite sex. Alvy as a child exclaims, "I was just expressing a healthy sexual curiosity," to which the precocious girl says, "For God's sakes, Alvy, even Freud speaks of a latency period." Alvy answers, "Well, I never had a latency period. I can't help it" (p. 8).

Critics of Allen recognize the importance of narrative desire to his work but see it as operating in the service of sexism and as perpetuating patriarchy. Thus, Richard Feldstein seems somewhat startled as well as disappointed in Allen when he writes: "Woody Allen's most celebrated film, *Annie Hall* was named for the female protagonist, a part for which Diane Keaton received an Oscar. In order to establish Annie's position, Allen encouraged the subject/spectator to identify with her, but only within the confines of narrative desire." Feldstein sadly notes that Allen remains at the center of the narrative in spite of the film's title:

Trace its code of narrative arrangement and you will find that *Annie Hall* is not about its namesake, because the primary sequence of events depicts Alvy's life, not Annie's. Although Annie is a historical subject who progresses through perceptible transformations, each passage is supervised by Alvy as part of his tutorial.[13]

For Feldstein, "Allen's use of the gaze" includes "Keaton within the intentionality of narrative design" primarily to "entrap the viewer in a cinematic look controlled by the apparatus." Allen's purported sexism in this interpretation is just part of his overall attempt through cinema to manipulate the spectator/viewer and control the experience and meaning of his films. Humor, usually at the expense of women, "mediates conceptualized lack," thereby radically taming humor's revolutionary potential.[14]

Feldstein's critical perspective of Allen as incorrigibly sexist, self-centered, and conservative remains consistent with the ideological stance that he establishes from the very beginning of his essay:

> In a world where Oliver North is viewed as a hero and Robert Bork promoted as an unbiased, even apolitical, nominee to the Supreme Court, it seems fitting that members of the liberal intelligentsia would celebrate Woody Allen as a man who loves and understands women. ...To believe such reviews, however, we must develop a convenient amnesia like John Poindexter's, allowing us to discount Allen's early films in which women become specular icons in a circuit of desire which repeatedly shifted its focus to the subject's scaffolding and the modern-day schlemiel that Allen invariably portrayed – a nebbish intellectually developed and verbally adept but sexually ineffectual if not absurd.[15]

The self-righteousness of Feldstein's rigid ideological position would seem to shatter the humorous drive behind Allen's work. Such criticism of Allen's place in American culture inevitably must exclude the subversive potential of his films. Seeing Allen's humor primarily as a means for imposing restraints upon the moral and political imagination of his audience, Feldstein maintains that even in his so-called avant-garde films, Allen only plays to widespread prejudices in a way that sustains sexism and the status quo.

The extremism of Feldstein's attack encompasses the range of radical perspectives on Allen's work. It also typifies how an important critical language and school can be used to discount authorial intent as well as opposing views. For example, disregarding the psychological and social dimension of Allen's characters and work, Feldstein's term "specular icons" suggests sexual confusion and paranoia; it reduces the complexity of Allen's film to a critical and ideological cliché and discounts Allen's experimentation with the subjectivity of the viewer. Feldstein's language indicates a repressive perspective that could include Botticelli, Michelangelo, and Rodin. In other words, in its failure to establish clear critical criteria between art and exploitation, this attack on Allen could be directed against many expressions of both female nudity and sexuality.

The self-centeredness that so offends some of Allen's critics is often a given in his work and a basic operating assumption in *Annie Hall*. In terms of the film's purposes and intentions, the firm adherence of *Annie Hall* to Alvy Singer's consciousness can be considered a major success. Starting with the opening monologue in which Alvy reveals his inner thoughts to the audience, the film inveigles the viewer into a position that supports the centrality of Alvy as the developing subject within the film's narrative.

Moreover, at the levels of both action and interpretation much of the movie sustains the ideas set forth in the monologue. As already noted, the narrative of the film works as a recapitulation of the end, both the end of their relationship and the end of the story. A story of memory and retrospection, *Annie Hall* dramatizes a return via narrative desire to the repressed and the unconscious in a manner similar to psychoanalysis.

Accordingly, more important than the rather obvious degree of Allen's narcissistic proclivities in *Annie Hall* are the explorations of various forms of subjectivity in the film through Allen's complex method of structuring narrative desire. Narrative desire in *Annie Hall* initiates and sustains a process of forming and then deconstructing the figure of Alvy Singer for the purpose of undermining the kind of privileged perspective and voice of authority that some critics see and hear in his work. The monologue that launches *Annie Hall* also instigates the special relationship between humor and desire that develops the modes of narrative in the film. In my view, visual and verbal humor give *Annie Hall* its force to subvert and reconstruct conventional modes of thought and gender constructions, which helps explain why radical critics of Allen often seem immune to his humor. In brief, Allen's humor energizes narrative desire to effectively invade conventional perceptions and experiences of reality and to explore new experiences and forms of creativity.

Allen quickly confronts the importance of narrative desire to his work by making immediate references to Freud and psychoanalysis. The strain of references to Freud and psychoanalysis throughout *Annie Hall* establishes a kind of metacommentary suggesting the power over narrative of the Freudian masterplot of the unconscious and desire. The perennial theme of Freud and psychoanalysis in *Annie Hall* constitutes a self-conscious assertion of how humor and narrative desire will work together in this film to break down and reform perceptions and ideas. Moreover, Allen's use of the relationship between Freud and humor forms a pattern of skepticism toward surface meaning that compels further interpretation. Just as a creative dialogue between the modes of *histoire* and narrative discourse forestalls closure, so Freud and psychoanalysis in Allen's film invite continuous reexamination and interpretation.

It is no accident that Woody Allen begins *Annie Hall* with a reference to a joke by Freud in *Jokes and Their Relation to the Unconscious,* ends it with another joke involving a psychiatrist and a patient, and in between includes innumerable allusions to and jokes about psychoanalysis. While these references indicate the pervasiveness of Freud in Allen's work, another joke provides an example of how humor and the unconscious relate and operate in the film. In the scene already mentioned in which Alvy and Rob walk down a Manhattan street, Alvy at first is heard but not seen rendering a Portnoyish whine about a presumed anti-Semitic remark. He says, "I distinctly heard it. He muttered under his breath, 'Jew'" (p. 9). Rob, of course, doubts Alvy and calls him "a total paranoid" (p. 9). "Wh – How am I a paran – ? Well, I pick up on those kind o' things. You know, I was having lunch with some guys from NBC so I said...uh, 'Did you eat yet or what?' and Tom Christie said, 'No, didchoo?' Not, did you, didchoo eat? Jew? No, not did you eat, but jew eat? Jew. You get it? Jew eat?" (pp. 9–10). The joke is funny in part because it casts doubt on all the participants. While the overly sensitive and highly imaginative Alvy dramatizes unconscious anxieties with his comment, Rob's resistance reveals his own tendency to avoid unpleasantness. Also, this joke demonstrates how Allen handles such a painful and controversial subject as anti-Semitism by both presenting and disarming it through humor. Throughout the film, Allen suggests the reality of anti-Semitism. The indirection of the joke softens the pain but heightens the reality of anti-Semitism by appearing to distance it from everyone except Alvy, while in fact the joke's very ambiguity encircles the other characters, the author, and the audience. The event described in the joke emanates from Alvy's deep-seated fears but touches everyone else as well.

The joke comes in the midst of a tide of Freudian references that suggests currents of unconscious drives and doubts: Rob's comment regarding Alvy's paranoia follows the opening joke about Freud; Alvy's revelation that "my analyst says I exaggerate my childhood memories" (p. 6), a judgment confirmed by Alvy's recollection of being raised underneath the Coney Island roller coaster; and the schoolgirl who scolds Alvy for failing to experience a latency period. It makes considerable sense for Allen to be fascinated by Freud since his humor and his interpretation of experience so clearly reflect Freud's insights into the relationship between jokes and the unconscious. Jokes are like dreams, according to Freud, because they give expression to disagreeable elements that are usually prevented from entering consciousness. In addition, jokes are structured by the same mechanisms that explain the operations of dreams. These mechanisms include condensation, which compares to the way metaphors relate different symbols and images, displacement, which operates like metonymy in associating one term for another one connected to it, and indirect representation, which suggests meaning through symbolic interpretation. Freud writes:

> We found that the characteristics and effects of jokes are linked with certain forms of expression or technical methods, among which the

most striking are condensation, displacement and indirect representation. . . . Does not this agreement suggest the conclusion that the joke-
work and dream-work must, at least in some essential respect, be
identical? . . . Of the psychical processes in jokes the part that is hidden
from us is precisely what happens during the formation of a joke in
the first person. Shall we not yield to the temptation to construct that
process on the analogy of the formation of a dream?[16]

Allen happily yields to precisely such a temptation in *Annie Hall* when
Annie relates to Alvy how she described a dream to her psychoanalyst: "In
– in . . . Alvy, in my dream Frank Sinatra is holding his pillow across my
face and I can't breath" (p. 61). Alvy associates her own singing with the
dream and represses the obvious meaning. However, Annie's psychoanalyst
already had hinted at the truth: "She said, your name was Alvy Singer" (p.
62). The shared processes of dreams and jokes merge beautifully as Annie
reveals one more aspect of her dream that also illustrates Freud's idea of
dreams as visual representations of words or ideas: "Because in the dream
. . . I break Sinatra's glasses" (p. 62). Alvy can no longer resist the meaning:
"Sinatra had gl – You never said Sinatra had glasses. So whatta you saying
that I – I'm suffocating you?" (p. 62). Even as Alvy confronts the truth, he
avoids and represses it with a joke that follows about Annie's implied desire
to castrate the singer in the dream.

Alvy's dramatic analysis of Annie's dream – dramatic because it evolves
through dialogue and a histrionic exchange of inner doubts and tensions –
constitutes an extremely original and effective model for interpreting the
film. In *Annie Hall*, Allen constructs scenes in a manner comparable to the
formation of dreams and jokes so that visual, verbal, and literary signs
function together to achieve a new complexity of meaning. Proffering visual
versions of condensation, displacement, and indirect representation, Allen
in *Annie Hall* devises a visual humor of great intelligence, originality, and
charm. He surpasses the humor of earlier films by developing a visual dimension for dramatizing the tension between manifest and latent meanings.
True, in many scenes the film serves merely as a stage for Woody Allen the
comedian to send forth verbal witticisms or gags – the merging of *Commentary* and *Dissent* into *Dysentery* (p. 27), his claim that "everything our
parents said was good is bad. Sun, milk, red meat, college . . . " (p. 30), the
analysis of Annie's dream just described, to cite just a few among innumerable other examples. Nevertheless, in scene after scene we get a visual
reinvention of reality through a humorous juxtaposition of hidden meanings
with external manifestations of desire. *Annie Hall* stands as Allen's so-called

breakthrough movie, what Graham McCann calls "a watershed," because Allen so creatively and so completely fuses his visual imagination to the verbal humor of the film's narrative. Also, Nancy Pogel writes, "What happens in *Annie Hall* is that we experience, more than in earlier Allen films, a feeling for the burden of history, the sophisticated self-consciousness, and the accompanying anxiety that contemporary people carry into their search for love, integrity, and meaning."[17] The visual inventiveness of the film dramatically and powerfully propels narrative desire to develop a complex art of many levels of interpretation. Thus, in terms of its radical approach to visual creativity and to the construction of gender and character, *Annie Hall* continues the artistic and intellectual advance achieved in *Play It Again, Sam.*

Some examples from early scenes in the film of Allen's visual imagination probably are worth mentioning immediately. The house under the roller coaster evokes a surrealist's modernistic rendering of contemporary insanity. The lineup of teachers in Alvy's remembrance of his school typifies a child's nightmare of a rogue's gallery of pedagogical torturers. Perhaps most interesting, visually speaking, is the famous Marshall McLuhan scene when Alvy and Annie stand and wait in a movie line. The annoyance of the line increases the tension between the couple as does the loud and pretentious discussion by a man in the line who harangues his companion with his opinions about movies. As a self-inflated and self-consumed intellectual, the man typifies a familiar target of Allen's ego-shattering humor. Like the scenes that preceded it of Alvy's youth and background, this scene also challenges a strict adherence to conventional cinematic realism. Not just the man in line, but Alvy and Annie as well speak too loudly. Alvy's running commentary on the conversation of the man would be overheard immediately – they are presumably so close that Alvy whines: "Well, he's spitting on my neck! You know, he's spitting on my neck when he talks" (p. 15). Any pretense of traditional realism ends when Alvy finally turns again to the audience: "What do you do when you get stuck in a movie line with a guy like this behind you?" (p. 16). In defense, the professor then also appeals to the audience. Thus, when Marshall McLuhan suddenly appears from off-screen to satisfy Alvy's desire for the ultimate authority with which to demolish the academic, the audience without realizing it has been set up for this wonderfully visual, but absolutely unbelievable joke. Moreover, as McCann notes, the importance of McLuhan's words derive from their utter incoherence: "What is so devastating about Marshall McLuhan's magical appearance is not his actual presence but the pathetic submission of the bore when McLuhan talks complete gibberish at him."[18] McLuhan says,

34

"You – you know nothing of my work. You mean, my whole fallacy is wrong" (p. 16). Such nonsense suggests our unconscious awareness of how all of us, but most especially academics, intellectuals, and even artists, including Allen himself, are vulnerable to public deflation and embarrassment as a consequence of pretensions and ambitions.

The scene with McLuhan also is important because its visual inventiveness – "the magical appearance" of McLuhan in McCann's words – conveys much of Allen's attitude and philosophy toward language and narrative. For Allen, language, even when used by a genius such as McLuhan, ultimately fails. In Allen's work, language is tentative and incomplete; it expresses void and absence in its most energetic attempts to achieve totality and wholeness. The most vigorous language becomes important for what it suggests of hidden thought and desire. Allen's dialogue, which we noted was cowritten in this case with Marshall Brickman, remarkably replicates the uncertainty of everyday speech, the pauses and gaps of deep insecurity and of latent fears and wishes. In contrast to a typical Hollywood drama, Allen's speakers constantly falter and verge on a stutter. For Allen, the truth clearly comes closest to the gap in language and speech. At the end of *Annie Hall,* we see a scene from a play written by Alvy about his relationship with Annie in which the actor and actress speak with a coherence, ordered syntax, and unity that are absent in the movie itself: "You're a thinking person. How can you choose this lifestyle?" (p. 102). And then we see Alvy smiling at the innocence and naïveté of his own work – "Tsch, whatta you want? It was my first play" (p. 102). Undermining the earnestness and false sincerity of the play within the play, Alvy's smile and "Tsch" speak volumes about the dangers inherent in inauthentic language and the difficulty of using language well. Even Alvy's opening monologue is constructed out of gaps, stutters, and pauses: "There's an old joke. Uh, two elderly women . . ." (p. 4). Other "Tschs" and "Uhs" and several "I, uhs" or an "I – I – I, uh" follow. Allen invents a stuttering poetics of insecurity, a poetics that suggests a world of unknown meanings and realities. Allen's humor renders and exploits this insecurity. The hilarity of the indefinite speech gets at least part of its charge from the gaps of confidence and certainty such speech suggests. Thus, Allen's dialogue manifests the kind of slippage and separation of meaning that Freudian students of language insist prevails in all discourse and signifying systems. Allen's visual inventiveness adds a deeper dimension to such slippage without creating an artificial or false coherence.

The dialogue between Annie and Alvy when they first meet exhibits such slippage and dramatizes the need for imaginative direction and visualizations to contribute to the rendering of their love affair. Significantly, this dialogue at their first meeting occurs after we already have met Annie and Alvy and know much about them as individuals and about their relationship. We have seen them argue in the movie theater and fight elsewhere as well as be affectionate together. And we have watched them go back and observe her relationship with a previous boyfriend as though viewing her past through their own personal camera, a technique used with extraordinary effect and poignancy later in the movie when they return with Rob to visit Alvy's family. Ironically, in the retrospective visit with Annie's old boyfriend, the young man talks in a rather sophomoric way about acting as "a visual poem" (p. 25), a metaphor that in fact can apply to Allen's own mature cinematic style. More important, the dichotomy that we discussed earlier between the actual order of events and the narrative order reinforces the inherent tension of uncertainty and the unknown in the film's visual and verbal language.

In the scene between Alvy and Annie under consideration, language becomes chaotic. Brilliantly acted by Diane Keaton and supported by Allen, the scene thoroughly disrupts and distorts coherent discourse. Signifiers and the signified are in complete disarray. Words and sentences are divorced from their apparent meanings. Yet although Annie and Alvy come close to a prelinguistic level of communication, only a matter of degree rather than kind separates the use of language in this scene from its use in other scenes. Upon seeing Alvy after tennis, Annie says, "Hi. Hi, hi," to which he responds, "Hi. Oh, hi. Hi," and she says, "Well...bye" (p. 31). After Alvy compliments Annie upon her tennis game, she fades into total confusion: "Oh, God, whatta – (*Making sounds and laughing*) whatta dumb thing to say, right? I mean, you say it, 'You play well,' and right away...I have to say well. Oh, oh...God, Annie. (*She gestures with her hand*) Well...oh, well...la-de-da, la-de-da, la-la." When Alvy then asks, "Uh...you-you wanna lift?" (p. 31), everything that follows means the opposite including which of them has a car and what direction they each are taking.

The difficulties with conversation persist in the following scene in Annie's apartment, the most conspicuous example being Annie's remark that her grandmother, Grammy Hall, would call Alvy "a real Jew" (p. 39). Annie seems totally oblivious to the insensitivity and impact of her words: "Yeah, well...you – She hates Jews. She thinks that they just make money, but let me tell yuh, I mean, she's the one – yeah, is she ever. I'm tellin' yuh" (p. 39). The vacuous nature of Annie's and Alvy's speech and conversation requires them to develop other means of communication to support any possibility for a meaningful relationship. In the earlier scene following the tennis game, visual support comes from Annie's distinctive style of dress, the wonderful body language of both actors, such as Keaton's brilliant physical depictions of insecurity, as well as other devices, including a phallic tennis racket in Alvy's bag that almost hits Annie in the groin. In Annie's apartment the visual support comes from Allen's engaging use of subtitles to convey Annie's and Alvy's inner thoughts. In a marvelous exchange about Annie's photographs, Alvy begins to sound like the academic he detested in the movie line. He starts to babble about the need for "a set of aesthetic criteria" to emerge from photography as a new art form, but his hidden thoughts consider "*what she looks like naked*" (p. 39). When Annie's innocent attempt to understand him deflates him with its honesty, Alvy suddenly looks nervous and his language grows truly pretentious and false. She says, "Aesthetic criteria? You mean, whether it's, uh, good photo or not?" meaning "*I'm not smart enough for him. Hang in there.*" He nervously answers, "The – the medium enters in as a condition of the art form itself. That's –" meaning "*I don't know what I'm saying – she senses I'm shallow*" (p. 40).

In these scenes, the vacancy of language requires Allen's visual imagination, not to add a false certainty or artificial truth to the scene, but to provide depth and breadth to the basic issue of presenting and articulating narrative desire. Both the subtitles and incoherent and disjointed dialogue dramatize the discontinuous nature of experience and the ineluctable tension between language and the unconscious in the attempt to organize and order experience. Visual representation and language place the unconscious in the very structure of the film in a way that suggests permanent destabilization and disunity.

At the same time, the film does suggest a degree of progress. Partly because of Alvy's influence upon her, Annie does learn to use language more effectively, at least in terms of achieving her independence and advancing her career. Annie's acquisition of more developed and coherent speech often evidences itself in rebellious exchanges with Alvy, a psychologically accurate way of relating her growth and her independence from Alvy. This relationship of language, power, and dependence is clear when Annie furiously responds to catching Alvy spying on her. She uses Alvy's own language against him: "Yeah – well, you wanted to keep the relationship flexible, remember? It's your phrase" (p. 59). Returning to school at Alvy's suggestion, she angrily corrects Alvy's childishly jealous attempt to belittle her when he misstates the title of her adult education course: " 'S – 'Existential Motifs in Russian Literature'! You're really close" (p. 60).

Accordingly, Allen's visual imagination in *Annie Hall* does not supplant linguistic and literary creativity. The visual and literary work together. One scene in the movie illustrates this process and works as a commentary on how the visual image and verbal expression complement each other in Allen's creative imagination. In this scene, *"it's a beautiful sunny day in Central Park,"* and Annie and Alvy observe the people and the events. In effect, we see the park through their combined vision. More specifically, the scene is so composed as to give the impression of looking through a stationary camera that captures everything that enters its view in absolute photographic and cinematic realism. However, Alvy's voice-over constitutes a running description of the action, events, and people – a commentary that turns what John Dos Passos years ago dubbed "the camera eye" into art: "Yeah, he's the Mafia Linen Supply Business or Cement and Contract, you know what I mean?" (p. 46). Perhaps it should be repeated here once again that although Allen coauthored the screenplay with Brickman, the marvelous combination of Allen's direction along with his work on the script makes this uniquely his film.

In the most powerful and significant moments of the movie, visual and literary modes advance *Annie Hall*'s complex narrative desire by repeating the story of the impossibility of completion and total unity. At one point in the film when Annie and Alvy temporarily reconcile following an anticipatory break in their affair, Annie says, "Alvy, let's never break up again. I don't wanna be apart," and he responds, "Oh, no, no, I think we're both much too mature for something like that" (p. 71). In point of fact, however, the film really is about precisely that – breaking up, being apart, and never overcoming emotional dependence and need. The breakups between people, between visual and linguistic signs and signifiers, and between the modes of narrative and *histoire* in our understanding of experience comprise the heart of *Annie Hall*. Several scenes are especially important in their suggestion of such separation. They mark the progress of narrative desire in the cinetext toward the final breakup of the lovers that Alvy pronounces at the very beginning of the film.

The complexity and impossibility of the human desire for total unity and completion comes through with humor and significance in the lovemaking scene in the country. Alone together in a country house, Annie mentions the possibility of going to a party: "Hey, listen, what-what do you think? Do you think we should, uh, go to that-that party in Southampton tonight?" Alvy, of course, resists, wanting her undivided attention and admiration: "No, don't be silly. What-what do we need other people for?" (p. 50). In effect, the situation dramatizes the dilemma of all lovers trying to incorporate the world within themselves and their relationship. Annie's instinctive resistance to such domination foreshadows their eventual breakup as does their mutual need for sustenance from others for their perennially impoverished egos. The separation of Annie's *"inner self, ghostlike"* from her body during lovemaking provides the startling and original visual personification of their incipient separation even in the midst of their most intimate moments with each other. Feeling Annie to be "removed" and "sort of distant," Alvy finally notices her "spirit" observing the couple in bed: "You see, that's what I call removed" (p. 51). Ironically, the scene following this acting out of existential separation and emotional distancing concerns Alvy's attempt to achieve wholeness in another area of his life by writing and performing his own material.

Alvy's success obviously attracts Annie and leads him into what probably stands as the movie's most famous scene of alienation and disunity – the Easter dinner at Annie's house so reminiscent of poor Alexander Portnoy's visit to the Campbells for Christmas in Philip Roth's *Portnoy's Complaint.* The opening line spoken by Annie's mother, beautifully played by Colleen Dewhurst, captures the milieu and values of the Halls' all-American suburban home and the family's latent social, class, ethnic, and psychological discomfort over Alvy's Jewishness: "It's a nice ham, this year, Mom" (p. 55). In this scene, Allen pulls out all of his visual and verbal stops. There is the image in Alvy's mind that instantly catches what he knows to be in Grammy Hall's mind – *"He is now dressed in the long black coat and hat of the Orthodox Jew, complete with mustache and beard."* Then, the failed attempt at humor in his response to Mom's reference to his fifteen years in psychoanalysis amounts to an expression of the guilt and loathing he assumes they feel toward him – "Yes. I'm making excellent progress. Pretty soon when I lie down on his couch, I won't have to wear the lobster bib" (p. 55). Of course, *"Mom Hall reacts by sipping from her glass and frowning. Grammy continues to stare"* (p. 55).

In this dinner scene, Allen once again violates traditional cinematic realism when Alvy directly addresses the audience to describe the family, a ploy that subtly conveys Alvy's psychological separation from the situation. His characterization of the grandmother as "a classic Jew hater" and his description of the family as the epitome of being American – again an interesting repetition of Portnoy's dilemma – helps to distance him from the hostile situation (p. 56). The address to the audience also establishes and then bridges the distance between Annie's and Alvy's families. Here, Allen inventively uses a split-screen technique to contrast the two families. The visual and verbal humor seems strongest when Mom Hall actually speaks to the people in the Alvy family frame. However, the humor operates according to the classic Freudian model already described as a disguise for latent aggressions and fears. With Alvy and Annie situated psychologically in the middle, the tension and differences between the indelicacy, exuberance, verbosity, and animation of the lower-middle-class Jews on one side of the screen as opposed to the reticent, tight-lipped, slightly inebriated, sterile chatter of Annie's all-Americans on the other side becomes manifest and palpable.

The presentation of Duane, Annie's brother, played with great skill and control by Christopher Walken, sustains and fulfills the impetus of the dinner scene. Duane's psychotic death-wish fantasy of an auto collision in which he has "this sudden impulse to turn the wheel quickly, head-on into the oncoming car" indicates that this family's external appearance of American gentility and reserve dissembles elements of tension and alienation that exist at its core (p. 57). Duane says, "I can anticipate the explosion. The sound of shattering glass. The . . . flames rising out of the flowing gasoline" (p. 57). Once again, Allen's visual ingenuity evidences itself in the next scene when Duane drives Alvy and Annie to the airport in a pouring rain. Annie sits smiling bemusedly, but happily between Alvy, whose facial expression shows utter desperation and anguish, and Duane, who drives with intense concentration, looking through creaking windshield wipers that exacerbate the tension. Obviously, death, insanity, and chaos are at the wheel while Annie seems oblivious to the situation and Alvy, feeling helplessly trapped, anticipates catastrophe. In one final, humorous shot that concludes this sequence, we go from Alvy's terrified face to the picture of Duane driving through a red light on this rain-soaked night. Fittingly, in terms of the development of narrative desire in the film, the next scene on a different day opens with a quarrel that clearly indicates the beginning of the end of Annie and Alvy's love affair. The power of the humor in all of these scenes to dramatically develop character and human relationships testifies to Allen's growth as a director and writer in this film.

Other scenes in *Annie Hall* are also important for visual and verbal originality. Juxtaposing scenes that humorously convey Alvy's contradictory attitudes and ideas, addressing strangers on the street about his affair, reproducing the love affair through cartoon animation, attempting to capture lost love with a woman who won't laugh over wandering lobsters, contrasting Hollywood's commercialism with New York's aesthetic creed, using the split screen again during Annie's and Alvy's separate therapy sessions to convey their conflicting perspectives on their relationship and to anticipate their impending breakup, suggesting the growing importance in Annie's life of a new love interest in the form of a rock singer, Tony Lacey – these all maintain the visual and dramatic originality of the film.

However, one scene seems especially important in its relationship to narrative desire in this film. This concerns the return of Alvy, Annie, and Rob to Alvy's family. Geographically they move into the different cultural and psychological environment of Brooklyn; but they also go back historically to an earlier time. The three physically enter into the world of Alvy's youth and family. In retrospect, they nostalgically visit parents, relatives, friends – a culture – long gone. The scene, which functions like a dream or fantasy, is cleverly constructed visually. In one room in the foreground, Alvy's parents fight over the problem of a black maid who apparently steals from them. In the middle of the frame, a young Alvy lies on the floor, feigning disinterest in this latest altercation between his parents. At the top of the picture in an adjoining room, the adult Alvy and his friends observe the whole scene. Alvy's physical bearing, actions, and facial distortions all clearly indicate the pain and embarrassment he feels over his embattled parents, a reaction that also powerfully implies the deep-seated, but hidden impact of the scene upon the younger Alvy. From a psychoanalytic perspective, the juxtaposition of the younger and older Alvy strongly suggests the permanent presence in our everyday lives of hidden forms of our infantile and adolescent past. Alvy shouts into the scene, "You're both crazy!" to which Rob responds, "They can't hear you, Max" (p. 73), using his personal nickname for Alvy. Perhaps the message amounts to little more than a Brooklyn version of "You can't go home again." However, it also can be argued that the visual power of the scene suggests more than mere nostalgia for the past. Allen renders a visual confirmation of his theme – disjunction, disunity, displacement. Placing narrative desire in the context of the relationship between *histoire* and discourse, the scene suggests the structural impossibility of desire's fulfillment.

In essence, by returning to the family toward the end of the narrative, Allen takes us back to the origins of desire. We see that the roots of Annie's and Alvy's desire emanate from an untouchable source in the past. This scene of return confirms the suggestion of the film's other family scenes of the permanent power of parental relationships over character formation. The family as an unconscious element of desire engenders the displacement onto the present and the projection toward the future of a past that remains forever disguised in receding signs and symbols.

Up to that point in his career, *Annie Hall* was Allen's most exciting and innovative exploration of the process of narrative desire. A considerable technical, artistic, and intellectual achievement, *Annie Hall* opened the way for other films in which Allen finally would break from the narcissism that so bothers some critics. With Annie as the visible object of desire, *Annie*

Hall from beginning to end focuses on Alvy's unappeasable desire, thereby confirming concerns about the masculine nature of narrative desire, even while Allen continues the project that he started in *Play It Again, Sam* of undermining conventional forms and structures of masculinity and femininity. However, in films that followed *Annie Hall,* the perspective broadens to include deeper appreciation for and understanding of other characters, both male and female, until he finally achieves an ultimate goal for himself, the making of great films about women.

Notes

1. Roland Barthes, *S/Z*, trans. Richard Miller (New York: Hill & Wang, 1974), p. 88.

2. For a further discussion of desire, see Sam Girgus, *Desire and the Political Unconscious in American Literature* (New York: Macmillan and St. Martin's Press, 1990), especially chaps. 1 and 2.

3. Teresa de Lauretis, *Alice Doesn't: Feminism, Semiotics, Cinema* (Bloomington: Indiana University Press, 1984), pp. 129, 121.

4. Ibid., pp. 111–12.

5. Woody Allen, *Annie Hall* in *Four Films of Woody Allen* (New York: Random House, 1982), pp. 4–9. All subsequent references to this film will be to this edition and will be included parenthetically in the text.

6. Peter Brooks, *Reading for the Plot: Design and Intention in Narrative* (New York: Vintage, 1985), provides a wonderfully coherent and thorough analysis of this approach to narrative, including an explanation of related terms, including those used frequently in contemporary cinematic discourse, *diegesis* and *mimesis*.

7. Ibid., p. 13.

8. Ibid.

9. Ibid., pp. 55, 37.

10. Ibid., pp. 104, 108.

11. Ibid., pp. 23, 215.

12. Ibid., p. 215.

13. Richard Feldstein, "Displaced Feminine Representation in Woody Allen's Cinema" in *Discontented Discourses: Feminism/Textual Intervention/Psychoanalysis,* ed. Marleen S. Barr and Richard Feldstein (Urbana: University of Illinois Press, 1989), p. 74.

14. Ibid., pp. 75, 84.

15. Ibid., p. 69.

16. Sigmund Freud, *Jokes and Their Relation to the Unconscious,* trans. James Strachey (1905; rpt. New York: Norton, 1963), p. 165.

17. Graham McCann, *Woody Allen: New Yorker* (Cambridge: Polity, 1990), p. 198; Nancy Pogel, *Woody Allen* (Boston: Twayne, 1987), p. 83.

18. McCann, p. 177.

3
Manhattan

Evil in the sense of willful and conscious malevolence usually does not intrude upon the worlds of Woody Allen. Probably not until *Crimes and Misdemeanors* does Allen engage forces of intentional harm and destruction. In *Annie Hall* the closest we get to such evil is the lobsters crawling around the floor and behind the refrigerator in Alvy's beach house in the Hamptons. Evil functions in *Annie Hall* as part of existential absence. It is structural, linguistic, and intellectual, but rarely felt as lived experience with the possible exception of crazy brother Duane. *Manhattan* also remains relatively free from malicious evil. Nevertheless, the film introduces a new degree of deception into a major Allen film. We soon learn that the characters in *Manhattan* frequently are not what they appear to be – which oddly enough represents many people's sense of New York, going back at least to the lonely excursions of Melville's distraught heroes into the inner depths of the city. Personal dishonesty and deceit are never far removed from all experience and relationships in *Manhattan*. Appearances of concern and commitment among friends only dissimulate latent jealousies, fears, and aggressions.

Although *Manhattan* examines a new moral dimension for Allen, it begins in a familiar place, the narrator's search for the right words. This search leads Allen to the creation of a visual panorama that literally explodes on the screen to the extraordinarily beautiful accompaniment of Gershwin's *Rhapsody in Blue*. On the surface, Ike's opening voice-over appears to be a humorous attempt to find a strong, individual voice to relate his story. Listening to him, we get inside his interior dialogue with himself as he projects an identity and then responds to it. Each attempt at such construction evokes humor because of its hyperbole. First, we get the hard-boiled voice of the experienced city dweller for whom New York existed "in black and white and pulsated to the great tunes of George Gershwin.'"¹ Then there is the self-described "romantic" for whom "New York meant beautiful women and street-smart guys who seemed to know all the angles" (p. 181). Then we hear the "preachy" editorializing that bemoans "the decay of contemporary culture" and the demise of "individual integrity" that was destroying "the town of his dreams" (p. 181). The preaching turns to angry denunciation of a "society desensitized by drugs, loud music, television, crime, garbage" (p. 182). Abandoning this tone, he settles on the most unrealistic self-description of all: " 'Chapter One. He was as ... tough and romantic as the city he loved. Behind his black-rimmed glasses was the coiled sexual power of a jungle cat.' I love this. 'New York was his town. And it always would be' " (p. 182).

With these words, one can envision the smile on Ike's face as he obviously feels successful in finding his voice. He seems to have achieved his goal of creating a transcending authorial power. In fact, of course, this opening achieves a very different effect of thoroughly undermining any transcendent authority. The interior dialogue does not build toward a final resolution of a single perspective or voice. Rather, it subverts the possibility for such a representative voice or singular vision. First of all, the interior voices operate against each other. This can be heard in the way Ike exclaims "I love this" in commenting on his own words regarding the sexual prowess of his hero. Obviously, Ike's glee reveals his identification with the character of his own creation. The humor in the scene derives in part from the way the gap between self-image and reality exposes the intensity of his desire, thereby dramatizing his vulnerability and denying the superiority of one narrative voice. This kind of critical counterstatement also can be found in the written text where the statement "I love this" stands without quotation marks in contention with the interior voice in quotation marks. Ike's comment on his own work – "I love this" – reveals one narrative voice in opposition to another in a manner that subverts the dominance of one particular voice. The words in and out of quotation marks engage in a democratic dialogue of multiple and competing voices.

In addition, the brilliant cinematographic display of New York combined with the startling sound track of the Gershwin *Rhapsody* graphically and dramatically serve to further diminish the authority of the discordant voices. The visual creativity and musical power literally overwhelm the voices. The wonderful flow of street scenes renders a city of power and excitement that radically contrasts with the utterance of Ike's spoken words and the fatuous excitement and self-inflation of his language. Instead of valorizing the narrative dialogue, the city scenes and the music engulf it. Similarly, the won-

44

derful conclusion of this opening sequence of fireworks that erupts over the magnificent New York skyline seemingly suggests some sort of climactic completion and victory of Ike's linguistic challenge to find an adequate single voice and identity for himself. The fireworks appear to celebrate not only the multifarious beauty of the city, but Ike's literary ambitions as well. This sense of visual confirmation of the narrative quest occurs on one's initial viewing of this scene because the cinematography is so exciting. In fact, the display also creates the opposite effect of undermining the narrator's attempt for unity. The explosion of fireworks shatters the pretense of conclusion and certitude. It marks a radical disjunction between the uncertainty of the voices and the power of the world around Ike. Attempting to construct himself as a strong subject in the midst of a mighty megalopolis, the narrator loses himself in the humor of his inadequacy. The fireworks, therefore, constitute the end of a series of visual and verbal contrasts and put-downs of the author. Coming at the conclusion of Ike's voice-over, the fireworks emphasize his insignificance. Thus, Ike does not find himself in his words, but creates a persona that loses itself in language. As the scene that immediately follows attests, he is no hero, no street-smart adventurer, no existential hipster on the dangerous and challenging avenues of urban conflict, no potent lover objectified into a "coiled sexual... jungle cat" by the glances of passing women of sophistication and beauty. Instead, we find him to be a representation of the fractured and fractious world around him, a person of warring parts, many of which are hidden from each other.

The theme of the insufficiency of words and speech to explain or structure experience carries over to the next scene at Elaine's, a popular Manhattan café frequented by intellectuals and artists. Indeed, the scene suggests that an overreliance on words and language perverts and distorts experience and character. Ike maintains "the important thing in life is courage," while his friend Yale Pollack advocates getting "in touch with feelings that you didn't know you had, really" (p. 182). Ike posits a moral dilemma of finding the courage to save a drowning person, but immediately escapes the necessity of dealing with his own issue by undermining it with a joke that dismisses the whole matter from serious consideration: "You know, I – I, of course, can't swim, so I never have to face it" (p. 183). The joke therefore inadvertently suggests that Ike is all talk; it reveals a quality of inauthenticity in Ike's character. His treatment of the issue also serves to alienate Ike from his audience. Yale's wife, Emily, drives home the point about the inadequacy of words without actions: "They've had this argument for twenty years" (p. 182), she tells Tracy, Ike's 17-year-old girlfriend.

The deeper point in this scene, however, continues Allen's debate with language in *Annie Hall*. Language, for Allen, externalizes and distorts. It signifies separation. In his first encounter with Mary, Yale's mistress, who will become Isaac's temporary lover, Isaac reacts with instinctive annoyance over her use of language when she explains a point by saying, "We believe in God." He says, "What the hell does that mean?...What is it – what – what'd you – what'd you – what'd she mean – what do you mean by that there?" (p. 195). However, this frustration with language manifests itself elsewhere in the film as it does in other Allen films. For example, later in a beautiful scene between Mary and Ike at the Hayden Planetarium ; teases her about her fixation on language and the intellect: "Because nothing worth knowing can be understood with the mind...you know. E – e – e – everything really valuable has to enter you through a different opening ...if you'll forgive the disgusting imagery" (p. 223). Indeed, Mary epitomizes people whom Allen regards as "well-educated and super-educated" to the point of being unable to deal with reality. In citing this comment made by Allen to an interviewer for *Time* magazine, Joan Didion attacks *Manhattan* for proffering a shopping center for emotions and prolonged adolescence.[2] In fact, Allen ridicules precisely such an attitude. Didion may be, as Graham McCann suggests, confusing Allen with his characters.[3] Throughout the film, Allen castigates a supermarket society of false values and artificial emotions. As Ike says toward the end of the film, "An idea for a short story" would consider "people in Manhattan who, uh, who are constantly creating these real, uh, unnecessary neurotic problems for themselves 'cause it keeps them from dealing with, uh, more unsolvable, terrifying problems about, uh, the universe" (p. 267). Even here, of course, Ike's words fail him because he remains very much a part of the problem. He exonerates himself, blames his friends, and ends his thought with the very sort of inflated and overly dramatic rhetoric that suggests the neurotic, self-created nature of his own problems. After all, he must share responsibility for his unhappy separation from the people he once loved. Also, his literal position in this particular scene – prone on a couch talking into a tape recorder, which functions as a substitute psychiatrist and secretary – suggests his own sickness as well as a surrender to dehumanized, mechanical forces he supposedly detests. The recorder embodies the physical detachment of speech and language as well as the absence of human connection during yet another moment of crucial need.

The visual counterpart to this kind of speech for Allen in *Manhattan,* of course, can be found in the highly innovative use of the Scope-screen. Indeed, the Scope-screen functions as a powerful visual metaphor for the world of inarticulate fragmentation and distortion that language renders. As Douglas Brode says:

> Nowhere in his films has Allen so brilliantly organized his frames. Whenever Isaac or any of the other characters come close to the realization that relationships are difficult to maintain, we see the character forced into one side of the Scope-screen frame. Sometimes, the remainder of the frame is filled with objects and clutter; at other moments, the remaining half of the frame is literally turned into a visual vacuum by the placement of some object which blocks everything else from our sight.[4]

In the beautiful opening scenes of New York that end with the fireworks display over the skyline, the Scope-screen conveys Allen's celebration of the breadth and magnificence of Manhattan. It suggests a kind of natural beauty and range to this unnatural urban setting.

However, when the scene fades and moves into Elaine's the potential of this visualization becomes even clearer. We are at a crowded table, in a crowded restaurant, in a crowded city. The very closeness is alienating and dehumanizing, the smoke and congestion stifling, in spite of Ike's antics with a cigarette. With the important exception of the angelic face of Tracy, played by Mariel Hemingway, the faces of the other characters become distorted and disproportioned as in a carnival mirror. Sometimes individual faces weirdly dominate the screen. Even the handsome face of Michael Murphy, who plays Yale Pollack, seems intrusive as it thrusts itself at the viewer, making the oxymoron of his name – the elite, WASP university and the ethnic association of his family name – into a palpable disruption. At other times, only half a face or a glass appears, illustrating further disruption. Indistinguishable parts of the anonymous bodies of café customers pass by the camera and block the view of the table. Furthermore, the banter and conversation are convivial and friendly, but the screen emanates a subtext with a different message. The picture, in a sense, is worth at least a thousand of the words of these people fooling each other. In this scene, we are also disturbed and embarrassed by the age difference between the 17-year-old Tracy and the 42-year-old Ike. Of course, Ike instinctively conveys his own discomfort by bringing attention to the subject: "I'm forty-two and she's seventeen. (*Coughing*) I – I'm dating a girl wherein I can beat up her father. It's the first time that phenomenon ever occurred in my life" (pp. 183–4).

The use of the Scope-screen grows increasingly more powerful and convincing as the film progresses. For purposes of this discussion, we almost could describe this visualization as the D-screen; it decenters, displaces, dislocates, and distorts. Through this technique, form and text become one with the film's ideological position of the psychological, social, and moral separation and isolation of the characters. The series of visualizations that are so persuasive and moving in *Annie Hall* are condensed into this visualization in *Manhattan* that operates so effectively throughout the film. The screen in *Manhattan* not only misplaces, loses, and hides characters, it also cuts them up into pieces. Tops of heads disappear, obviously indicating mindlessness, and legs are fractured, suggesting a grouping of truncated grotesques. People talk to invisible listeners or are observed by unseen eyes. Cripples of the physical and moral kind inhabit this visual island, this cinematic synecdoche of a sick society. As Allen himself has said, "*Manhattan* is about the problem of trying to live a decent life amidst all the junk of contemporary culture – the temptations, the seductions."[5]

Allen exhibits his strengths as a director through his employment of the Scope-screen in different and original ways throughout *Manhattan*. Collaborating creatively with both his photographer, Gordon Willis, and his co-writer, Marshall Brickman, Allen continuously invents different uses for the Scope-screen for the scenes that comprise *Manhattan*. Even minor, relatively undramatic scenes are visually interesting in their development of important verbal or literary aspects of the film. Thus, as the two couples leave Elaine's, Yale and Ike walk ahead of the women on the street and Yale confesses his affair with Mary. As Yale provides details of his dark secret in hushed tones so that Emily won't hear, we notice that they walk in darkness and shadow on sidewalks barely illuminated by streetlamps. When Yale and Emily are alone in their apartment, the screen exaggerates the close quarters; it frames and thereby targets Yale as Emily questions him, and it allows the couple to hug on the left edge of the screen, abandoning the center and suggesting an irregularity in their relationship.

In the following scene, Meryl Streep, who plays Jill, Ike's lesbian first wife, emerges from the revolving door of the impressive Time–Life Building as a powerful, beautiful, and dynamic presence, long, blonde hair draped luxuriously over her left shoulder. She walks briskly and the camera tracks her, ultimately placing Ike, who is lurking in a doorway to question and challenge her over a forthcoming book about their marriage, within the frame. She doesn't break her stride as they exchange cryptic comments. The tracking continues so that the physical motion becomes an accelerated externalization of the psychological energy behind the verbal exchanges between Streep and Allen. When they do stop to talk, it is before pulsating, shooting fountains of water, suggestive of their failed sexual relationship, an image and idea reinforced by the dialogue that ranges over Ike's spilling "wine on my pants," his concern over his son being raised by Jill to "wear dresses," and her mocking comment: "Look at you, you're so threatened" (p. 188). As she walks off, his parting words vent his frustration and anger: "Hey, I'm not threatened because, I, uh, of the two of us, I was not the immoral, psychotic, promiscuous one. I hope I didn't leave out anything" (p. 188).

In the next scene between Ike and Tracy in Ike's apartment, Allen further reveals the potential of the Scope-screen as a cinematic and visual means for developing character, human relationships, and psychological and social conditions. The scene participates in a clear and intelligent progression of scenes that continually narrow our focus on Ike's life and character. The screen positions him ever more specifically in terms of space from the great opening view of the world of Manhattan, to his closest relationships and friends, to his actual living space. It does this, however, without sacrificing the consistency of the Scope-screen as the visual embodiment of displacement and decentering. The Scope-screen visually dramatizes the condition of desire or the sense of detachment between internal and external experience. The closer the Scope-screen takes us to Isaac and his most intimate relationships and most comfortable environmental spaces, the more alienated and detached he becomes. Allen exploits the screen to convey two contradictory conditions, separation and distance even in confrontation with their opposite, connection and involvement.

Thus, in the apartment scene with Tracy, the visual image conveys Ike's internal psychological state and social situation by positioning him with great care in his home. We learn an enormous amount about him here simply by seeing his place or, in this case, absence of place. The scene makes explicit what before had only been implied. First of all, we see the important signs of his professional success. The apartment obviously qualifies for the upwardly mobile, even to the point of having two levels of living space connected by a spiral staircase – going in circles? – as the border and pillar for the right end of the screen. Large, expensive, and stylishly decorated, the apartment provides a properly fashionable living space for a creative personality and successful television writer like Ike. The range of the Scope-screen captures the essence of the apartment and, in so doing, the internal landscape of a way of life. While the staircase to the right is bathed in light, at the other end of the screen the living room is relatively dark with one lamp and a light emanating from an adjoining room. Such lighting and contrast between dark and light spaces unsettle the scene, helping to establish the mood of separation and distance. In contrast, Tracy sits comfortably

49

on the couch, apparently at home in what are obviously familiar surroundings. However, she seems barely distinguishable as a person in this setting. Behind her a wall of bookspace and bookcases dominate the scene, as Alvy's books about death and despair buried Annie. We can just about find her from the sound of her voice. Ike approaches from the staircase on the right, almost coming from another world. In between them, a gray wall that hides the kitchen stands out as a kind of dead space on the screen.

This visualization of dislocation dramatically contradicts and undermines the ostensible feeling of cozy familiarity between Ike and Tracy. Their conversation in this scene also sustains the visual theme of separation, while the distance in their ages dramatizes differences of feeling and commitment. Tracy asks, "Well, don't you have any feelings for me?" (p. 189). Ike tries to tell her that because of her youth, she has to keep her options open: "You've got your whole life ahead of you" (p. 189). Then in a painfully transparent expression of his own doubts, he says, "I've got nothing but feelings for you, but, you know ... you don't wanna get hung up with one person at your age," even though he adds, "It's ... tsch, charming you know, and (*Clearing his throat*) ... erotic. There's no question about that. As long as the cops don't burst in, we're – you know, I think we're gonna break a couple of records ... you know" (p. 189). Ironically for being situated on a screen of dislocation, their talk is all about using and sharing space. She wants to stay in the apartment – just as Annie initiated the idea of sharing an apartment with Alvy – and develop their relationship, while he clearly wants space, space that we already have described as alien and decentered. He says, "You should think of me ... sort of as a detour on the highway of life. Tsch, so get dressed because I think you gotta get outta here." The directions make the vigor and insistence of this wish seem even stronger than the rather crude expression "gotta get outta here." "(*He gets up from the couch and takes Tracy by the hand.*)" She appeals, "Don't you want me to stay over?" (p. 189). As the scene ends, they walk up the staircase holding hands and exchanging teases about popular culture and age difference. On the one hand, it is charming. On the other hand, the Scope-screen has helped to expose a whole dimension of meanings and feelings.

As in the opening sequences of Manhattan and the skyline, the Scope-screen also expresses extraordinary beauty. This is generally considered to be the case for the presentation of the evening when Ike and Mary meet at a party and stay together to walk and talk. They end up together on a bench by the 59th Street Bridge, looking over the river and watching the sunrise. Undoubtedly, this is a moving and effective scene. Douglas Brode thinks it is perhaps the movie's strongest moment: "In the film's most unforgettable

Figure 2. Diane Keaton as Mary and Woody Allen as Isaac Davis greet the morning by the 59th Street Bridge in *Manhattan*. (United Artists)

image, Mary and Isaac grow deeply involved with one another on a wistful New York late-night interlude."[6] The musical background of "Someone to Watch Over Me" helps make the scene irresistible and wonderfully romantic. However, even here, Allen's genius for undercutting appearances with a disruptive, hidden reality of dissociation manifests itself. In the film, the exciting bridge arching over the river occupies the center of the frame, creating a strong sense of balance and symmetry with Ike and Mary at the lower right and an enormous eyesore of a structure dominating the middle of the left of the screen, between the bridge and the surface (Fig. 2). Interestingly, in both Brode's book and the book of Allen film scripts, not only is the latter structure absent from the photo duplication of this scene, but Mary, Isaac, their bench, and her dog Waffles are much closer to the center of the shot, presumably to make the picture fit onto the page.

How radically different are these versions of the same thing. The abbreviated picture shows a cozy couple in an intimate setting with the bridge overflowing the entire upper left part of the frame. For me, the film version creates a very different effect, also beautiful, but conveying a whole other set of potential meanings. The couple and the dog are dwarfed by an imposing, extraordinary force of great physical power and thrust. The vertical structure on the far left beyond the bridge harshly disrupts the visual harmony and contributes to the feeling of disjunction about the couple. Moreover, the visual frame is stationary. We never see the couple engaged in their conversation, but only hear their voices since their backs are to the camera and the viewing audience. In addition, their sudden sense of personal engagement occurs in the context of what we already know about them and the relationships and experiences they bring to this romantic moment. Given the history we already have of their personal and romantic failures and violations – his with a teenager and hers with a married man – this new emotional bond offers little immediate promise of anything more than a momentary connection to fill in gaps of discontent and loneliness. Just as the bridge itself arches off into a distant fog and haze, so also one envisions a relationship ultimately going nowhere.

In this regard, the bridge itself has its own significance. Not the Brooklyn nor the George Washington nor even the Verrazano of *Saturday Night Fever* – New York's most famous bridges – the connection this bridge makes to a seedy part of the borough of Queens would be beyond the knowledge of most viewers, perhaps even most New Yorkers who are more familiar with other routes. At the same time, others might recognize it as Gatsby's bridge to the Valley of Ashes and death. It is the bridge on which he encounters death in the form of a hearse, a bridge to oblivion. Ike's words have a distant echo of *The Great Gatsby*, even if it melds into a Borscht circuit version of Fitzgerald's story: "Well, my book is about decaying values. It's about... See, the thing is, years ago, I wrote a short story about my mother called 'The Castrating Zionist.' And, um, I wanna expand it into a novel" (p. 212). Even the song that provides additional background, "Someone to Watch Over Me," puts the mystery of the bridge in the place of the famous advertisement of old Dr. T. J. Eckleburg's eyes, especially when one further considers how the film later will deal directly with issues of God, morals, and man. Accordingly, the scene entails a perfect prolepsis of ultimate failure.

At least as exciting visually is another scene between Mary and Ike at the Hayden Planetarium, where once again Allen exploits the Scope-screen to express the decentered and displaced nature of experience. Here, the universe – or at least the part of it that the great planetarium by Central Park can contain – becomes the metaphor for the human condition as lived by Ike and his friends. Allen therefore achieves a kind of ultimate positioning of Ike, taking him from the midst of Manhattan to a series of apartments and then expanding his world again to the solar system, making Mary and Ike into little planets of their own, a lovely conceit for the "culture of narcissism." The Scope-screen renders their existence as such planets in darkness, shadow, and reflected light. Their presence then socializes the world of the planets into the human situation. However, the planets move according to laws of nature and astronomy, following very precise mathematical formulas. In contrast, these people are propelled by far more mysterious, hidden forces of human emotion and desire. They have met at her urging to fill up an empty Sunday of missing Yale, whose marital obligations have forced him out into the suburbs. They flee into the planetarium's protection of darkness from a sudden thunderstorm that has dashed their impulsive hopes for a walk in the park.

Intellectually the scene probably never escapes the confines and limitations of the rather obvious – perhaps even trite – comparison between bodies in space and bodies of desire yearning to establish a human dimension of feeling, commitment, and love. At the same time, the scene still provides a powerful visual dramatization of the film's major themes of decenteredness and displacement. Thus, as Isaac and Mary – whose very names suggest religious and ethnic distance from each other – walk into the interior of the planetarium, they move from well-lit anterior rooms into the darkness of outer space exhibits. Visually they become part of outer space. "*Silhouetted in the darkness by a huge illuminated photograph of a nebula,*" they can barely see each other. In the darkness, Mary, worried about the effect of the rain on her appearance, asks, "How – how do I look?" (p. 221). Ike's simple answer, "I can't see" (p. 221), does not inhibit him from quickly adding, "You look kind of nice, actually. You're sort of pretty," thereby raising questions of beauty, perception, and distortion in this and other scenes. Allen directs a dance of light, shadow, and space to indicate the difficulty involved in establishing emotional contact with one's self and others in a world in which psychological blindness contributes to disguise and distortion. For Allen, of course, that blindness often originates in unconscious forces and sexual ambivalence.

In the preliminary stages of what will be a short-lived affair, Mary and Ike deal with each other at the planetarium as distant objects, shadows in an alien, frozen universe in which nothing human could live. The Scope-screen becomes the perfect vehicle for exhibiting and dramatizing such absence and distance. Total blackness takes us into one frame. Then we see a moon exhibit, a moonscape *"realistically portrayed with its craters and rock sculptures"* (p. 221). We do not see the couple at all, but hear only voice-overs, Mary revealing her true thoughts at the moment concerning Yale: "You know, I'm really annoyed with Yale" (p. 222). A brilliant moon moves to the left, taking over three-quarters of the screen, top to bottom. Out of the darkness emerges Ike and Mary, talking about the costs that accrue from secret affairs. Tellingly, Mary finishes a sentence that Ike starts. He says, "Well, you know, that's what happens when you're –," and she immediately interrupts, "I know, when you're having an affair with a married man." She thrusts her next sentence at Ike, indirectly sharing her secret doubts about herself and her illicit affair: "What a terrible way to put it." Ike defensively indicates that her statement really constitutes an act of self-condemnation: "Hey, I didn't put it that way" (p. 222). While Mary and Isaac continue to talk about her marriage to a man who in turn cheated on her, a stranger with a camera enters the Scope-screen and comes between the couple and the audience, pauses, bends slightly at the knee, and takes a picture in the direction of the audience. The vagarious intrusion adds an element of additional distance to the scene. The stranger's own face is divided by shadow, reiterating the darkness from which Ike and Mary speak. The camera serves as an obvious prop symbolizing the objectification of vision and images.

As the couple continues to speak and walk, their darkened bodies seem like shadows following the voice-overs that add to the fragmentation of mind and body. It is at this point by the Saturn exhibit, when Mary has been putting on an exhibit of her own factual knowledge of the satellites of Saturn, that Ike basically belittles her by trivializing such information, telling her of the uselessness of the mind: "Nothing worth knowing can be understood with the mind" (p. 223). Once again, the film blackens, emphasizing the abyss not only between people, but of a philosophical and linguistic kind as well between mind and body and between verbal and visual signifiers and what they signify. From off-screen Mary says, "I know, you – you probably think I'm too cerebral." They walk through a tunnel of total darkness, their bodies finally catching up with their voices, until Ike stops at the dead end left of the screen, facing off-screen to hear an invisible Mary describe him as having "a tendency to get a little hostile, but I find that attractive" (p. 223). Walking through these dark and gloomy exhibit corridors, Mary overcomes this momentary lapse from her obsession with herself to return to her fear of being unable to relate mind and emotion: "So you think I have no feelings, is that it?" (p. 223).

Allen's direction here maintains a visual choreography of light, darkness, shadow, and space to convey emotional, psychic, and human distance and inconstancy. He concludes the scene with a light but brilliant touch that particularizes this visual choreography. Speaking in whispers, Ike and Mary are face to face. They are shown in profile, almost touching, their faces bathed in darkness and silhouetted against a photograph of the stars. They are finally intimate, discussing Mary's insecurity and oversensitivity. The subtext of the conversation clearly concerns Mary's loneliness and desire for companionship in the absence of her true infatuation, Yale. First, she suggests some dinner and Ike says, "I gotta see somebody this evening." Then she suggests a meeting next week: "Right. Well...so what about sometime next week? I might give you a call or – Do you have any free time?" Again, Ike prevaricates, "Uh...I'm – I'm not gonna have – I don't think I'm gonna have any free time, you know, 'cause...," quickly adding, "I don't think it's such a great idea for me. I'm, you know, I'm working on this book" (p. 224). A subsequent scene that evening between Ike and Tracy reveals that Ike in fact had no plans. He resists Mary's overture primarily out of loyalty to her lover and his friend Yale, a seemingly noble gesture. Yet the little lie, which is only secondarily related to his ambiguous commitment to Tracy, perfectly underscores the visualization of distortion and deception at the planetarium.

The theme of deception finds even stronger reinforcement in the scene between Yale and his wife immediately following the planetarium. Returning from Emily's parents' home, Yale's voice-over resonates with grating arrogance as the camera follows the couples' car over the George Washington Bridge and the Henry Hudson Parkway: "Well, your parents were in a good mood. I almost had a good time" (p. 224). Emily then asks, laughing with her husband, "Who was that you called after dinner?" Of course, it has to be a call he made to Mary. He uses his lie about the call as a way to tell another lie in order to see Mary that night. Only his hesitation and stutter suggest his duplicity: "Oh, uh, uh, Da – David Cohen. He wants me to review the new book on Virginia Woolf. He's written another one. Can you believe it?" Gullibly, she does and accedes to his next lie: "Listen, I told Cohen I'd stop by and pick up the book. Is that okay with you?" (p. 225). In any event, the lies both Ike and Yale tell to women make a perfect verbal commentary upon the visualizations at the Hayden Planetarium of darkness and distortion that Allen engineers on the Scope-screen.

Toward the end of the film, the Scope-screen structures a climactic visualization of distortion and deception when it alternates between two scenes involving Mary, Ike, and Yale. Perhaps these scenes provide the film's most graphic visual demonstration of displacement and decentering through the innovation of the Scope-screen technique, which Allen employs to create a kind of visual narrative of deception. He interweaves these very brief scenes meticulously into the very heart of the film's characterizations, themes, and plot development. The scenes emphasize spaces at the ends of the screen within the dramatic contexts of the situations, thereby powerfully illustrating the absence of a stable center in both social and psychological relationships. The scenes also emphasize the idea of alienation I have been calling displacement. The sense of homelessness in the form of the absence of a solid position from which to construct identity and subjectivity pervades these moments in the film. Interestingly, a verbal lie once again accentuates the visual portrayal of deception. Ike and Mary are working separately at opposite ends of his new apartment and the Scope-screen. Instead of working together, sharing their individual tasks in a collective way, they occupy separate spaces, almost separate compartments. As he lies on his bed writing and she types in the living room, they communicate through open door space and thin apartment walls. The visual image exaggerates the separateness and detachment since they still can hear each other talk and work to some degree. The image thus dramatizes the psychological and emotional isolation of their situation.

The scene shifts from left to right and back again as they talk. On the left side, Ike is seen through a half-open door to the right of which is another door and then a block of space that further separates him from Mary in the living room. The effect is one of extreme fragmentation. The doors jut out as does the cigarette in Mary's mouth. The block of wall space is an inherent eyesore and inevitable frustration. As he talks, we hear her typewriter confirming our assumption of poor communication between them, especially since she speaks to him in a near shout. Also, she is framed into the work space in a perfect rectangle, a geometric space resembling prison confinement. In fact, she seems more than crammed into the space, but literally crushed by the oppressive gray space.

The apartment exudes an unsettling, impinging atmosphere in terms of both physical space and personal interaction. Even the relatively minor distraction of the jingling telephone adds to the general disorder. Of course, when we realize that the call comes from Yale, the discomfort increases considerably, largely because the picture of him sneaking back into Mary's life and breaking up his friend's life so effectively fulfills the film's expectations. Appreciating the questionable nature of his call, Yale obviously feels relief that Mary rather than Ike has answered the phone: "Mary, hi. It's Yale. I was hoping you'd pick up. Listen – uh, could we meet for coffee?" (p. 255). The cut to Yale making the telephone call is perfect. The thrust in the film toward decentered lives finally has succeeded in making Yale just about invisible. We hear Yale talking to Mary, but we see a Park Avenue street scene from the vantage point of the intersection. The only immediately visible presences are the people crossing the street. Then we realize that to the extreme right of the screen must be Yale in his own prison of the phone booth that stands inconspicuously on the corner. The telephone booth is so narrow and so removed from the center of the frame, which concentrates on the street, that it seems ready to be pushed off the end of the screen. I say Yale must be using this telephone booth because he in fact remains only barely discernible. The camera never closes in on him. We see the profile of a man wearing glasses holding a phone over his ear in a way that offers further concealment, adding even more to the suggestion of deceit and hiding. Mary's lie to Ike when she hangs up the phone that the call was a solicitation for "free dance lessons" (p. 255) registers pain and confusion on her face. Ike, of course, stays in the dark, so to speak, unaware of the meaning for his future of the apparently petty annoyance of the call. The brief scenes engender a pointed visual summary of the fragmented and alienated relationships of the film.

Allen develops another visual irony by virtue of the Scope-screen that adds to the potential impact of Mary's loss upon Ike. This visual image constitutes a comic use of the Scope-screen and immediately precedes the phone call in the apartment. In this scene, Ike's confidence over his relationship with Mary gets a boost after they accidentally encounter Mary's ex-husband, Jeremiah, in a clothing store. Throughout the film, Mary has proclaimed the brilliance and the sexual prowess of this man. Now after finally meeting him, Ike can gloat over perceiving him as "this little homunculus" who should offer little competition to him in terms of intellect or sexual potency and agility (p. 254). While Mary and ex-husband chat, Ike moves off-screen to observe. Although totally outside of the frame, the obvious presence of his look renders the scene very funny. However, the sensitivity and originality of Allen's direction prevents the scene from deteriorating into a mere sight gag. Ike's confident bubble of superiority soon will burst when his affair takes its inevitable course toward deception and failure. This adds both irony and pathos to the encounter with Jeremiah, a comic prophet of Ike's eventual exile from the screen as far as Mary is concerned. As Brode says, "There is only one sight gag in the movie: When Isaac and Mary (Diane Keaton) go rowing in Central Park, he leisurely lets his hand drift in the water, then finds it covered with a murky pollutant." Moreover, the visual humor as represented by the Jeremiah scene is consistent with the humor throughout the film. As Brode, again, and many other critics have noted, in *Manhattan* "comedy and drama are completely fused."[7] The humor here contributes significantly and coherently to the development of character and theme.

Equally important, the humor maintains Allen's focus on psychic and social fragmentation, while also sustaining dramatic dialogue. Examples abound of this effective use of verbal humor as a means to support the powerful visual images of the film. Telling Ike that Jill and Connie can raise Ike's son without any problems, Mary says, "Uh, they made some studies I read in one of the psychoanalytic quarterlies. You don't need a male. I mean, two mothers are absolutely fine, just fine." Ike answers, "Oh, really? Because I always feel very few people survive one mother" (p. 208). When Mary confesses that even though she was sleeping with Jeremiah when he was her professor, he still gave her an F, Ike says, "No kidding. Not even an Incomplete, right?" (p. 210). As they return home in a taxi from dinner, Ike says self-deprecatingly to Mary, "You look so beautiful I can hardly keep my eyes on the meter" (p. 243). After learning from Mary about her renewed feelings for Yale, Ike confronts Yale, who inadvertently reveals that in fact he has been meeting with Mary: "We met twice for coffee" (p. 265). Ike fires back, "Hey, come off it. She doesn't drink coffee. What'd you do, meet for Sanka? That's not too romantic. You know, that's a little on the geriatric side" (p. 265).

The great paradox of *Manhattan* is that beneath the wonderful structures of the skyline and the complex, sophisticated lives of the characters seethe rather banal but cruel forms of unfulfilled desire seeking expression in generally twisted, distorted, and destructive ways. The pyrotechnics of Allen's directing, cinematography, visual images, and engaging humor provide the surface presentation of the internal source of fragmentation and displacement – sexuality and the unconscious. Visual creativity and the integration of humor and drama structure the film's narrative of a series of love relationships that engender division and displacement. While the Scope-screen and the precisely integrated humor dominate the surface events of *Manhattan*, narrative desire continues to propel Allen's development as a director and writer. Truly, Allen has learned and grown from everything he has created and studied. The love stories in this film, therefore, derive from the relationships in *Play It Again, Sam, Annie Hall,* and *Interiors* and pave the way for *Hannah and Her Sisters* and *Crimes and Misdemeanors.* As Allen told one interviewer about *Manhattan,* "It's like a mixture of what I was trying to do with *Annie Hall* and *Interiors.*"[8]

Accordingly, the innovative visualization and imaginative dramatization of narrative desire in *Annie Hall* achieves even greater visual and literary complexity and originality in *Manhattan*. Rather than developing one narrative consciousness and voice and constructing one subjective position as in *Annie Hall*, in *Manhattan* Allen drastically broadens the arena of desire to several different characters and relationships. As McCann says, "Perhaps the most significant fact about *Manhattan*'s construction is its elliptical treatment of Allen's own character: simply, less time is needed to register the meaning of Isaac's actions and personality."[9] It is not, however, so much that Isaac is treated more elliptically than Alvy, but that Allen uses Isaac to create a more complex subject and field of multiple voices and perspectives within a vital and persuasive social, psychological, and artistic context.

Like Alvy in *Annie Hall*, Ike's character structures narrative desire in *Manhattan*. However, *Manhattan*'s Scope-screen presents multiple relationships that anticipate the libidinal exuberance and erotic complexity even of *A Midsummer Night's Sex Comedy*. Through these characters, Allen explores the nature of desire itself. Just as the camera shots and images present destabilization and displacement, so the characters and relationships in *Manhattan* establish a diversity of voices and subjects related to desire. In other words, Allen achieves a dialogic exchange of characters and positions that sustains the multiplicity of his visual imagination. Visual diversity and complex characterizations function creatively together. In doing this, Allen creates an ideology of form that adds film to Mikhail Bakhtin's notion of the fluidity of the social and linguistic. Bakhtin intends, of course, to reveal the contradictory and oppositional forces inherent in all hegemonic ideological systems. "The study of verbal art," he says, "must overcome the divorce between an abstract 'formal' approach and an equally abstract 'ideological' approach."[10] Bahktin's emphasis on utterance and the social context of voice that imbues a complexity of meanings to speech and words relates to Allen's penchant as a director for voice-overs and the separation of bodies from speech, as well as his own dialogic technique of overlapping speech and running words together. Indeed, it could be argued that Allen therefore typifies Bakhtin's concept of the "carnivalistic," which concerns the annihilation of rigid boundaries in communication and human relationships.[11] This carnivalistic quality pertains from the very beginning of the film when, we recall, Ike attempts to find a single, coherent narrative voice, but instead really creates an extraordinary dialogue of voices.

Allen's "dialogic imagination" in *Manhattan* continues his project that began in *Play It Again, Sam* of reconsidering, revisioning, and reconstructing sexual ideologies. While narrative desire encompasses and structures the concerns of all his characters in *Manhattan,* male and female, the intensity and pertinacity of the process of decentering in the film moves the focus of desire from the single male consciousness of the character played by Allen to the other characters. A multiplicity of male and female voices and perspectives operate to fulfill dialogic expectations. In effect then, *Manhattan* becomes a study of desire in which the complex issues related to desire of sexuality, masculinity, femininity, and gender roles resist closure and go beyond the film's inconclusive ending. Positioning these issues within the broad range of the urban setting as presented on the Scope-screen, Allen particularizes them by developing a series of relationships between several couples in the film.

It is important to recognize these as relationships of desire, situations of psychic displacement rooted in the unconscious, as opposed to the humorous sexual exploits that are played mostly for laughs in his earlier works. These relationships are Ike and Tracy, Ike and Mary, Yale and his wife, Emily, Yale and Mary, Jill, Ike's ex-wife, and her lover Connie. In addition, the intense male bonding between Yale and Isaac remains implicit and important in the subtext. With so many relationships, the structure of narrative desire in *Manhattan* must necessarily differ from *Annie Hall,* where a kind of structured chaos organizes narrative desire as the story breaks conventional temporal and spatial patterns. However, in *Manhattan* Allen artfully parallels the progress of these relationships, moving carefully in and out of them. He interweaves the subnarratives to construct the larger narrative that comprises the movie. Together they entail the Freudian master narrative of desire, the unconscious, and retrospection.

In essence then, the visual presentations of emotional and social situations in *Manhattan* are rooted in the democracy of desire. The inherent instability and precariousness of sexual organization continually disrupt the relationships of desire in the film, constructing a radical dialogue of desire in which the most basic questions about love and identity are asked but never answered with finality. Allen holds the film together through a careful interweaving of pairings that in themselves suggest a complex sexual ideology because the pairings are both volatile and in tension with each other. Inherently unstable and disruptive, the relationships are capable of exploding into a sexual and emotional chain reaction of pain and loss. Thus, these relationships incorporate an ideology of uncertainty and indeterminacy into the very structure of *Manhattan* just as the Scope-screen also constitutes an ideology of form.

Mary Wilke, played by Diane Keaton, is the major female figure in this film that includes several important women. She also is the most unstable and disruptive. Indeed, her uncertainty regarding sexual choice and love probably establishes the paradigm for sexuality in *Manhattan*. When Ike tries to dissuade her from leaving him to go back to Yale, he says, "And – and – and if he does commit to you, you know, when you start to feel secure, you'll drop him. (*Snapping his fingers*) I know it. I – I give the whole thing...four weeks, that's it" (p. 262). She answers honestly, "Well, I – I – I – I can't plan that far in advance." Ike instinctively casts her as crazy and paints himself as the victim, resisting the implication of his own words of a pattern in his behavior toward women for which he must ultimately assume responsibility: "You can't plan four weeks in advance? I mean, what –...– what kind of foresight is that? (*Sighing*) Jesus. You know, I – I knew you were crazy when – when we started going out. I – you know, I...y – you...always thinking you're gonna be the one that makes 'em act different, you know, but...eh" (p. 262).

Mary, however, is more than merely flighty. What Ike at this moment in the film attributes to her "crazy" capriciousness and lack of commitment, forgetting in the process his own lack of credibility and moral strength, actually typifies the social and psychological state of love and sexuality in their part of Manhattan. It is no accident, I think, that the meeting between Ike and Mary that marks the beginning of their friendship, after two initally hostile encounters, takes place at a party in support of the Equal Rights Amendment at the Museum of Modern Art's sculpture garden. Especially because this event includes the appearance of Bella Abzug, the radical feminist and New York personality as a guest speaker, this party at first viewing seems like an effort by Allen to be stylish, as in the casual reference to Jack (Nicholson) and Anjelica (Huston) in *Annie Hall* that Joan Didion derides as pretentious in her review. Actually this gathering at the museum helps to put the sexual turmoil of the film within a social context. It demonstrates Allen's concern that *Manhattan* occurs during a time of social and sexual transition when definitions of gender and patterns of relationships are themselves in confusion. The importance of feminism as a theme in the movie receives further impetus when Yale, speaking of Mary, tells Ike, "Yeah, well, she's – uh, very active in the feminist movement" (p. 212).

Of course, Yale's comment can be taken ironically. Mary's relationship to feminism remains largely problematic in the film. Indeed, her efforts to achieve legitimacy and authority as an intellectual and individual graphically dramatize obstacles facing women of both a psychological and social sort that still obtain. Her attitude toward herself as illustrated dramatically by her self-consciousness about beauty emphasizes such internal and external obstacles. Walking with Ike after the museum party and before going on to the 59th Street Bridge to greet the sunrise together, Mary expatiates vituperatively on the trials of being pretty: "Uh, you'll never believe this, but I never thought I was very pretty. Oh, what is pretty anyway? I mean, I hate being pretty. It's all so subjective anyway" (p. 208). She then elaborates upon her feelings about how looks remain the top priority for a woman in a man's world: "I mean the brightest men just drop dead in front of a beautiful face. And the minute you climb into the sack, if you're the least bit giving, they're so grateful." Of course, Mary internalizes the very ideology of beauty and desire that she denounces. At the planetarium, as already noted, her first thought concerns her appearance. Similarly, when Yale finally decides at one point to end the affair because of fear ("And I don't wanna break up my marriage and then find out – that we're no good together"), Mary retreats to her beauty as her first line of psychic defense: "Of course I'm gonna be all right. What do you think I'm gonna do, hang myself? I'm a beautiful woman, I'm – I'm young, I'm highly intelligent, I got everything going for me. The point... the point is – is that, uh, I don't know. I'm all fucked-up" (p. 232).

Both Ike and Yale confirm Mary's ideas in their feelings not only toward her, but toward all women, as when Ike notes that he married Jill in spite of warnings from his analyst about her lesbianism: "Yeah, I know, my analyst warned me, but you were so beautiful that I – that I got another analyst" (p. 217). Not learning from his mistake, Ike, when he takes his son Willie to lunch at the Russian Tea Room, overcompensates for his insecurity regarding his ex-wife and teaches the boy about the importance of beautiful women to a man: "They have very beautiful women that eat here. You know, we could – we could do very well. I think we could've picked up these two if you were a little quicker. I'm serious. I think the brunette liked you" (p. 219). Similarly, Yale finds Mary's beauty bedazzling. At a rendezvous at Bloomingdale's department store, Yale kisses and flirts with her. She halfheartedly resists: "This is – it's just ridiculous. It's – you're married. I can't... Listen to me, I'm beginning to sound like I'm one of those women. I – it sounds terrible. I hate it" (p. 213). She adds, "I'm – I don't want to break up a marriage yet" (p. 214). Still, she proves vulnerable to Yale: "God, you are so beautiful" (p. 214). It turns out that she also can be bought at Bloomingdale's with a little flattery and the appearance of passion and affection: "Can't you just hold me? Does your love for me always have to express itself sexually? What about other values, like warmth and spiritual contact? A hotel, right? Jesus, I'm a (*Laughing*) pushover anyway" (p. 214).

To other shoppers at Bloomingdale's, the illicit relationship between Ike and Mary might seem fairly commonplace. However, in the midst of the flirtatiousness, Mary interjects a comment that suggests how her attitude also affects other aspects of her life. Attitudes and values about sexuality and gender ultimately influence and help structure her career and work as well: "Oh, did I tell you? I think I may have an interview with Borges. I – I – I told you that we met before when he was here. And he seems to feel very comfortable around me" (p. 214). Her remark reveals her own lack of regard for her work by treating it incidentally. It is of secondary importance to maintaining Yale's interest in her. Her work involves not her own writing, but her secondary status as an object that can manipulate men by letting them "feel very comfortable around me" – in other words, by allowing herself to be used by them in turn. Also, the phone call from Yale at Ike's apartment that will lure her back into their affair comes during a conversation in which Ike appeals to her to stop writing "novelizations of movies." When he asks her why she does it, her answer indicates a great deal: "Why? Because it's easy and it pays well," while his response suggests how much in fact she loses through such work: "I mean, you're much too brilliant for that. You know, you should be doing other stuff" (p. 255).

Mary's avowed feminism fumbles and fails before the depressing pattern of her obsequious relationships to men, from Jeremiah, the "homunculus," through Yale and even to Ike, to an extent. At times, she reduces her sense of incompletion without men to psychosexual categories, as when she describes her dachshund as "a penis substitute for me," to which Ike predictably jokes, "Oh, I would have thought then, in your case, a Great Dane" (p. 209), and when she complains, "My problem is I'm both attracted and repelled by the male organ" (p. 241). While both comments are clearly meant to be taken humorously, from a psychoanalytic point of view they intimate a basis in the unconscious to her narcissism and dependency. The film's running joke about her analyst, a man she familiarly refers to as "Donny," who does drugs and calls on her at times for counseling and help, does not diminish the film's insistence on Mary's need to internalize values that will strengthen her to become her own person rather than an object of others' desires. Mary emerges as an important character who embodies a serious dilemma in a world that still resists the social and personal challenge to construct serious alternatives for the independence of women. Even in the absence of achieving true individuality, she gains a voice and presence in the film that Annie Hall probably never attains. Moreover, her voice comes at Ike's expense, a subtle undermining of the kind of central consciousness that dominated *Annie Hall* through Alvy.

Mary's situation of dependence upon men complements the position of

Emily who is totally restricted in the film by her role as Yale's wife. In an impressive visual touch that dramatizes this theme of gender roles and women's position in society, Emily is seen picking up newspapers around Yale when he tells Ike on the phone of Mary's commitment to feminism. The visual irony of Emily's domestic subservience and Yale's arrogant deceit and abuse follows an earlier scene in which she attempts to gain a commitment from Yale concerning her wishes to move to Connecticut and have children. Yale's refusal on both counts leaves her nothing. Understandably, then, Emily is the least developed and least interesting of the women in *Manhattan*. She stands as a kind of negative extreme. However, she also represents an oppositional force against which to compare the other characters, especially Tracy, who sits with her and Yale and Ike at Elaine's at the beginning of the film. As noted earlier, the viewer instinctively shares Ike's blatant discomfort and embarrassment over his relationship with a girl young enough to be his daughter. He volunteers, "She's got homework. I'm dating a girl who does homework" (p. 185). However, it seems to me that Allen cultivates this obstacle of discomfort over a questionable relationship to create a truly original character, a young woman who becomes a blending of romanticized feminine adoration, vulnerable innocence, and unselfish sophistication.

Allen clearly intends to propose Tracy as a product of contemporary culture, someone beyond the experience and sexual guilt of his own generation. She teases him by feigning ignorance of the difference between Veronica Lake and Rita Hayworth: "Do you think I'm unaware of any event pre–Paul McCartney or something?" (p. 190). When he condemns the extramarital relationship between Yale and Mary as being opposed to his own values and upbringing, she modernizes his viewpoint. He says, "Well, I'm old-fashioned. I don't believe in extramarital relationships. I think people should mate for life, like pigeons or Catholics." She responds with a maturity that remarkably almost silences him. She also voices an important theme of *Manhattan* of sexual liberation as a confusing force in contemporary society: "Well, I don't know, maybe people weren't meant to have one deep relationship. Maybe we're meant to have, you know, a series of relationships of different lengths. I mean, that kind of thing's gone out of date." He responds, "Hey, don't tell me what's gone out of date, okay? You're seventeen years old. You were brought up on drugs and television and the pill. I – I – I was World War Two. (*Sighing*) I was in the trenches" (p. 197). Smiling, Tracy helps him with his math ("Oh, you were eight in World War Two"), as she will again later in the movie when Ike attempts to establish some distance between them by trying to figure out how old he will be when she turns 36 (p. 226). She tells him. Characteristically, Tracy sees right through Ike's words and excuses when he tries to end their relationship to begin one with Mary. "Have you been seeing someone?" she says, adding, "You keep stating it like it's to my advantage when it's you that wants to get out of it" (p. 245). He responds, "Hey, don't be so precocious, okay. I mean, don't be so smart."

Of course, Tracy is even smarter. Sexually uninhibited and aggressive, she also feels more comfortable than the others with her emotions. In spite of her modern ideas about the impermanence of relations, Tracy wishes commitment, further suggesting qualities of maturity and complexity to her character. Early in the film, she says, "I think I'm in love with you," in the context of asking him about his feelings toward her (p. 189). However, when Ike announces the breakup, she becomes most insightful in the midst of the genuine pain he causes her: "I can't believe that you met somebody that you like better than me" (p. 246). Her hurt, but dignified response to Ike's words contrasts with Mary's vindictive, distraught profanity when she gets a similar message from Yale (p. 233).

Based on her honesty and commitment, the prescience of Tracy's comment about love will ultimately haunt Ike like a curse. Her love, as he realizes at the end, comes closest to being the true one for him. However, it is true only in a thoroughly idealistic and narcissistic sense. Reality, thereby, also proves Ike correct because the love with Tracy cannot be realized. Intelligent, intense, and insightful, Tracy nonetheless still remains impossible. At the end of the film when the memory of "Tracy's face" returns to Ike as a major force that makes life worth living, we hear echoes of his earlier description of her on their horse-drawn carriage ride by Central Park (p. 268). We also discern, by the way, a return to Gatsby in the form of the "disembodied face" of Daisy Buchanan that motivates Gatsby to such dreadful and extraordinary pursuits. Ike says to her, "You – you – you're . . . look, you're – you're God's answer to Job . . . you know. You would've ended all – all argument between them. I mean, H – H – He would've pointed to you and said, you know, 'I do a lot of terrible things, but I can also make one of these,' you know. . . . And then – then, Job would've said, 'Eh, okay – well, you win' " (p. 227). Fittingly for such a moment in the park, Ike buries his head in her shoulder and kisses her hand – almost as Gatsby might have done.

Ike neglects to tell Tracy that this concocted conversation involves patriarchal figures interested in a woman for their pleasure and glory. Similarly, Tracy epitomizes Ike's desire. I think her ultimate disavowal of this role suggests that Allen indeed may be proposing her as a symbol of freedom and love in the future, as did Hawthorne with Hester Prynne. As the end of the film makes clear, she must resist such objectification. Indeed, the wonderful shot of her through the glass door as she combs her hair in anticipation of leaving for London personifies such desire. The glass door, reflections, and glimmerings all contribute to this effect. Ike's visual gaze represents classic cinema's masculine look of desire. Interestingly, a bar on the door decapitates the image. Such desire can kill her. The intensity of Ike's desire, his selfishness in trying to keep her from going to London because of his sudden whim, his previous dishonesty, and his weakness in pursuing the dream all insist on Tracy's need to achieve her own identity and fulfill the potential of her mind. Tracy must continue on the path Ike in fact helped her to find toward maturity and independence, thereby helping to reverse the situations of Mary and Emily. The final gaze of the camera turns on Ike himself in all his incompleteness and uncertainty, perhaps placing the mantle of desire on his own shoulders. Thus, *Manhattan* cannot promise fulfillment or completion for either Ike or Tracy, but it can reject dependency and mindlessness.

In comparison to the position in society of the other women in *Manhattan*, Jill seems the most marginalized, although she shares with all of them an existence as the object of masculine desire. As a lesbian mother raising her son with the help of her companion Connie, her purpose in the film at first appears to be to make Ike feel and look weak and ridiculous. In the film's geography of desire, she exists as an alien on the fringe. Her moments on the screen are indeed brief, making for an unfortunate waste of the enormous presence and power of Meryl Streep. Yet such brevity replicates her place in the society itself, which is that of a figure whose sexuality tends to ban her from the vision of others. It comes as an irony, therefore, to realize that the thrust and structure of narrative desire in the film is toward her. For example, in the scene at Bloomingdale's when Mary concedes to Yale's sexual overtures and she describes herself as a "pushover anyway," the film fades to Jill and Connie at home, the important visual point being that here are no pushovers. The point takes a sharper edge in the immediate conversation when Ike arrives to take his son out and responds with surprise that Willy likes to draw since neither parent draws. Connie says, "I draw" (p. 215). Suddenly the margin shifts to include Ike rather than the women. Ike's efforts to insert himself back into the middle by persisting with the question "I can't understand how you can prefer her to me?" (p. 216) or by demeaning his wife's relationship with Connie by asking if Willy wears dresses (p. 188) only succeeds, of course, in further diminishing his stature. Jill, as already noted, says, "Look at you, you're so threatened" (p. 188). Jill also asks one question that resonates through all of the relationships between men and women in *Manhattan*: "Do you think we can be ever just friends?" (p. 217). The film answers with a resounding no, not under the situation and conditions between the sexes that the film depicts. Thus, Jill's most important act of independence, other than making her own decision regarding her choice of lover, indeed constitutes an act of hostility toward Ike, writing her book about their relationship. The book's success contrasts purposefully with Mary's failure to ever achieve a comparable act of independence. With some real justification, Ike feels embittered over the negative publicity the book engenders. However, the movie clearly suggests that his sense of threat existed long before the public exposure of the book. Ike's fear and failure of both imagination and understanding obviously derive from his own ambivalence and uncertainty and make any kind of resolution impossible. The violence of his initial reaction to the relationship between Jill and Connie is another one of the film's running jokes. Apparently, Ike at one point tried to run over Connie with his car, a charge he has persistently denied: "Uh, do you – do you honestly think that I tried to run you over?" (p. 260). Jill asks back smartly, "Well, what would Freud say?" and he answers, sealing his own fate on the question, "Freud would say I really wanted to run her over. That's why he was a genius" (p. 260).

As usual in Allen's movies, the resort to Freud should not be taken lightly. It reopens the whole question of the relationship of sexuality, desire, and the situation of women in the film. Thus, Yale's comment to Ike about his influence on Jill also has pertinence here. He says to Ike that "under your personal vibrations, she went from bisexuality to homosexuality" (p. 238). Resistance to that complexity regarding sexuality and desire helps account for the vision and the pervasiveness of displacement and decentering in *Manhattan*. The movie suggests that in matters of desire and sexuality, there are no simple answers. Moreover, the complexity also must include the friendship of Ike and Yale. Yale uses Ike to defend his decision to Emily against moving to Connecticut: "What about Isaac? I mean, we can't abandon him, you know. (*Chuckling*) He can't function anywhere other than New York, you know that. Very Freudian" (p. 187). The Freudian connection, however, might include Yale's dependence upon Ike as well. When Ike defends Yale against Mary's recriminations about being misled by him, she says, "You guys all stick up for each other" (p. 235). Also, Ike refers to Yale as "family" just prior to learning this "brother" plans to take back the old girlfriend (p. 256). Ironically, Ike's loyalty to Yale seems to take precedence over other relationships. Initially, it keeps him from seriously dating Mary. It prevents him from being honest with Emily about Yale's affair, a situation that later keeps him from protesting and correcting Emily when she admits she has blamed him for the breakup of her marriage because of his introducing Mary and Yale to each other. It forces him to apologize with embarrassment for his affair with Tracy before he had dealt with the implications of that affair for himself. His anger over Yale's duplicity at least equals if not exceeds his pain over losing Mary. Two special relationships have been violated through their betrayal of him.

Isaac's harangue against Yale about morals and commitment at the end of the film should be understood in the light of Ike's own actions, especially his attempt in the final scenes to regain Tracy. The words are powerful and correct, but Ike cannot separate himself from their meaning. Just as playful triteness runs through Ike's opening of the film, so a good deal of self-serving cant finds its way into his concluding speech to Yale. After being told by Ike that "you're too easy on yourself," which of course happens to be absolutely true, Yale says, "You are so self-righteous, you know, I mean, we're just people, we're just human beings, you know. You think you're God!" Ike only half-jokingly responds: "I – I gotta model myself after someone!" (p. 265). Probably the more realistic model stands next to Ike in the form of a skeleton. Thus, Ike's comment, after gesturing toward the skeleton, that "this is what happens to us! You know, uh, it's very important to have – to have some kind of personal integrity" contains its own explosive irony. Actually, the skeleton also makes the opposite point – the futility of searching for moral absolutes and privileging one's own moral authority; for the absence of integrity in the sense of wholeness and completeness has been apparent throughout the film.

Lacking a program and prescription to guarantee such moral perfection, the film offers instead a dialogic exchange of voices and perspectives that not only breaks the hold of a single person's privileged position of moral superiority but also gives expression to alternative voices and contending visions. It uses the visual renditions of fragmentation and incompletion to present the uncertainty of psychic and social existence. And it argues that even as divided people and cultures, we must address the moral dimension of experience. In its reconsideration of these issues, it also proposes a vision of reconstruction for the future from which to find a foundation for further building. It does all of these things with extraordinary artistic fusion up until the very end of the film when Ike says, "Tsch. W-well...uh, ah, do you still love me or – or what?" and Tracy answers, "Do you love me?" (p. 270). Her final words are, "Not everybody gets corrupted...Tsch. Look, you have to have a little faith in people" (p. 271). Love, faith, the promise of failure, and the existential and moral demand to continue the effort to be human conclude the film in the midst of the knowledge that, ironically, most people deserve precisely just "a little faith."

Not your typical Hollywood ending, the concentration of the camera on Ike's sad face provides the film's perfect final image of vulnerability as the sounds of *Rhapsody in Blue* return. With Gershwin's music once again engulfing the film, Ike's ambiguous smile beautifully epitomizes the tension of desire and despair. Initially a source of desire, he ends as its victim, a reflection of Tracy's imminent absence darkening his smile. We have gone full circle. The search in the beginning of the film for subjectivity, voice, and identity concludes with Ike silent and empty, but also perhaps educated and somewhat changed. The thrust of the movie toward vision, beauty, and desire results in a visual surgery of Ike, a psychic cutting of himself that casts him with the women of *Manhattan* as a symbol of unfulfilled desire. The god of desire – the original "castrating Zionist" – that creates Tracy's face also cuts Ike's throat by silencing him again. The dialogic exchange ends as it began, with Ike lost in Gershwin. His journey, however, has made him pregnant with possibility.

Notes

1. Woody Allen, *Manhattan* in *Four Films of Woody Allen* (New York: Random House, 1982), p. 181. All subsequent references to this film will be to this edition and will be included parenthetically in the text.

2. Joan Didion, "Letter from Manhattan," *New York Review of Books*, August 16, 1979, p. 17. See Frank Rich, "An Interview with Woody," *Time*, April 30, 1979, pp. 68–9.

3. Graham McCann, *Woody Allen: New York* (Cambridge: Polity, 1990), p. 101.

4. Douglas Brode, *Woody Allen: His Films and Career*, 2nd ed. (Secaucus, N.J.: Citadel, 1987), p. 198.

5. Ibid., p. 196.

6. Ibid., p. 194.

7. Ibid., pp. 191, 187.

8. Ibid., p. 188.

9. McCann, p. 206.

10. M. M. Bakhtin, *The Dialogic Imagination: Four Essays*, trans. Caryl Emerson and Michael Holquist (Austin: University of Texas Press, 1981), p. 259.

11. M. M. Bakhtin, *Problems of Dostoevsky's Poetics*, trans. Caryl Emerson (Minneapolis: University of Minnesota Press, 1984), pp. 122–3.

4

The Purple Rose of Cairo

Poststructural Anxiety Comes to New Jersey

Woody Allen gave the *New York Times* a fairly straightforward explanation for the genesis of *The Purple Rose of Cairo.* He told Eric Lax, "After working on one thing for a while, and for a while is one film because that takes a year to do, you want to do something different. I had just made *Zelig* and *Broadway Danny Rose,* and I thought this was a different kind of movie. I thought it would be interesting if a character came off the screen." Allen goes on to say how the film came together for him as a concept:

> The thing that really started to cement it for me was I realized that in addition to all the ensuing complications of that, there would be an actor playing that character. Once it occurred to me that it would be part of his problem, too, and that I had a totally fictional character and an identical real character, I thought there was enough substance to do a film that I hoped would be entertaining and also about something: the difference between fantasy and reality and how seductive fantasy is and how, unfortunately, we must live with reality, and how painful that can be.

Allen adds that this contrast between fantasy and reality provides the necessary "elements" for a successful film: "I thought it had good elements to it: comic elements, surreal elements, farcical elements. I thought it was material that it would be worth it to work a year on."[1]

With some important exceptions, which I will discuss later, most critics were ecstatic about *The Purple Rose of Cairo.* Vincent Canby of the *New York Times,* who had called Allen "America's most authentic, most serious,

70

most consistent film auteur," hailed the film in both his initial review and his follow-up essay several weeks later. In the review, Canby said:

> To be blunt about it, *The Purple Rose of Cairo* is pure enchantment. It's a sweet, lyrically funny, multi-layered work that again demonstrates that Woody Allen is our premier film maker who, standing something over 5 feet tall in his sneakers, towers above all others.

In the review, Canby noted that Allen's technique of having a character come alive off the screen encourages him "to rank it with two acknowledged classics, Luis Buñuel's *Discreet Charm of the Bourgeoisie* and Buster Keaton's *Sherlock Junior,* both of which it recalls though in no way imitates." Canby further maintained that the film also "recalls" some of Allen's early fiction, namely "The Kugelmass Episode," a very funny story about a professor who loves Madame Bovary so much that he enters into Flaubert's novel with extraordinary results.

Like other reviewers who were excited by the movie, Canby also praised the acting of the cast, including Mia Farrow, Jeff Daniels, Danny Aiello, Dianne Wiest, Van Johnson, Edward Herrmann, among others, as well as the contribution of Gordon Willis, the director of photography, and Stuart Wurtzel, the production designer. In the subsequent longer piece, Canby added a more comprehensive view of Allen's development as a director up to *The Purple Rose of Cairo:*

> With *Zelig, Broadway Danny Rose* and *The Purple Rose of Cairo,* Mr. Allen has managed to achieve – with seeming effortlessness – the kind of comic destiny he demonstrates in his best prose stories and sketches. He has mastered his own, very particular kind of movie making, which, unlike writing or even doing a stand-up act in a nightclub, is an immensely complicated collaborative endeavor involving other actors and highly skilled technical artists on the order of Gordon Willis, his favorite cameraman.[2]

With the benefit of hindsight, it seems to me that *The Purple Rose of Cairo* is every bit as important as Canby says, but that calling it "enchanting" misnames the force that makes the film so compelling, while Allen's description of it in relatively obvious terms as emphasizing the contrast between fantasy and reality understates its underlying complexity and brilliance. However, before proceeding with a discussion of this film, it is necessary to detour briefly to one of the earlier films Canby mentions, *Zelig,* as a prelude to the cinematic innovation of *The Purple Rose of Cairo.*

The propelling force behind *Zelig* and *The Purple Rose of Cairo* is Allen's fascination with film and the cinematic image. Like *Play It Again, Sam* and *Stardust Memories,* they are not just movies about movies, but self-conscious efforts to include in their very form some of the artistic, psychological, and intellectual issues related to films. Allen, as many critics have noted, strives to understand the processes by which films mediate and validate experience. Films, he suggests, often provide the terms and categories for seeing and understanding life. Allen continues this examination in *Zelig,* which was constructed largely from fragments of history recorded on film.

In *Zelig,* as in *Take the Money and Run,* Allen uses a mock documentary form to tell the story of Leonard Zelig, the human chameleon, whose desire to conform and gain acceptance from others causes him to take on the attributes and traits of the people around him to the point of becoming black around African Americans or instantly acquiring the technical skills of associates and acquaintances such as doctors, dentists, musicians, and pilots. The technical wonder of the film, which owes much to earlier innovators such as Orson Welles in *Citizen Kane,* derives from the extraordinary expertise through which Allen as Zelig becomes integrated in a seemingly inexhaustible number of events and situations from meeting major sports heroes to distracting Adolf Hitler during a Nazi rally. As Graham McCann says:

> The technical brilliance of *Zelig* is undeniable: Allen has *engrained* himself in the old movie images. Fitting into fifty-year-old frames, Zelig appears to hug Josephine Baker and James Cagney, pose alongside Eugene O'Neill and Calvin Coolidge.[3]

Zelig's desire to be loved epitomizes the American dream and has inspired some critics to pursue the Gatsby theme in Allen's work. Jack Kroll of *Newsweek* called Zelig "the Great Gatsby as schlemiel," while Douglas Brode notes that "Woody insists on the Gatsby connection here by beginning and ending the film with quotes from Scott Fitzgerald."[4]

As these references to Gatsby suggest, the sociological impetus behind *Zelig* is fairly apparent and by itself could, in fact, reduce the film to a truism or oversimplification about contemporary alienation and angst if it were not for the film's technical originality and ultimate aesthetic triumph. The film's wonderful documentary footage of social life and activity during the 1920s, all with Allen's Zelig at the center or margins of the scenes, contributes brilliantly to this sense of social history. Indeed, such eminences of the New York intellectual scene as Irving Howe, Susan Sontag, Saul Bellow, and Bruno Bettelheim articulate this social interpretation. Integrating these figures into the movie as a clever means of sustaining the documentary motif, Allen uses them to deliver the social message of *Zelig*. Thus, Bettelheim, the famous psychoanalyst, says, "I myself felt that one could really think of him as the ultimate conformist."[5] In one truly touching scene fairly early into the film, the running joke about Zelig as the human chameleon takes a serious and pathetic human form when we see Zelig sitting by himself in a chair, munching on a roll, crossing and uncrossing his legs. The gray and white tones of the scene accentuate its jarring mood and highlight the feeling of loss and desperation in Zelig's character. At this juncture, Zelig the joke becomes an object of genuine pity and concern. The narrator's voice-over, which provides structure for the entire film, directly addresses Zelig's existential condition as a nonbeing as well as his social condition of total alienation:

> Zelig's own existence is a non-existence. Devoid of personality, his human qualities long since lost in the shuffle of life, he sits alone quietly staring into space, a cipher, a non-person, a performing freak. He who wanted only to fit in – to belong, to go unseen by his enemies and be loved – neither fits in nor belongs, is supervised by enemies, and remains uncared for. (p. 56)

Suddenly, Zelig takes his place along side other embodiments in American literature and culture of the alienated man and outsider lost in a hostile urban setting that go back to Poe's "Man of the Crowd" and Chaplin's tramp.

Allen also follows this theme of alienation and the mass man to its natural conclusion, his perennial obsession with Hitler and Nazism, subjects that appear in *Annie Hall* and *Manhattan,* among other films and works. After a temporary triumph over his malady of nothingness, Zelig again collapses into conformism and the existence of a chameleon and flees, only to be ultimately discovered as part of Hitler's entourage at a rally in Munich. Saul Bellow explains the point in a mock interview that parodies conventional sociological jargon and critical analysis:

> Yes, but then it really made sense, it made all the sense in the world, because, although he wanted to be loved . . . craved to be loved, there was also something in him . . . that desired . . . (*Pauses*) immersion in the mass and . . .

As Bellow continues to speak, the documentary shows how "*Zelig as Fascist stands among Hitler and the Nazi soldiers.*" Bellow concludes his interview noting that "anonymity, and Fascism offered Zelig that kind of opportunity, so that he could make something anonymous of himself by belonging to this vast movement" (p. 115).

Zelig is followed across the ocean to Hitler's Munich rally by Dr. Eudora Fletcher, played by Mia Farrow. His wife and therapist, Dr. Fletcher, who was responsible for his early but temporary cure, spots him at the rally behind a gesticulating Hitler and attracts his attention. In a remarkable and wonderfully funny scene, Hitler literally interrupts his ranting and turns around to berate Zelig for disrupting the speech to wave to Eudora. It is an extraordinary fulfillment of the entire method of the film.

Equally interesting, just at this point of Hitler's rage, the film cuts swiftly to a Hollywood version of the event. Thus, Allen makes a parody of a Hollywood movie about Zelig within *Zelig*. This demonstrates that at the technical limit of one device – the integration of Allen and Farrow into real documentary footage of Hitler and the Nazis – Allen immediately can muster another technique that he used before and will use again, the film within the film. Such technical versatility and dexterity not only comment on Allen the director, but also suggest a subtextual theme of the power of the media itself, especially as it can be used for propaganda and destruction by fascist forces. Zelig and Eudora make their Hollywood-ending escape from the pursuing Nazis by capturing a plane, which Zelig flies upside down across the Atlantic, breaking the world's record for such a flight. A patriotic and jubilant America greets them to see living proof of the validity of Zelig's earlier messages about being your own man and finding your personal identity:

> You have to be your own man and learn to speak up and say what's on your mind. Now maybe they're not free to do that in foreign countries but that's the American way. You can take it from me because I used to be a member of the reptile family, but I'm not anymore. (p. 94)

Of course, the film questions the possibility of ever being "your own man."

Going beyond the image of the faceless mass man in the mass society, the film develops the key relationship between Dr. Fletcher and Zelig as an intriguing combination of therapy and love that cannot be separated from the film's concern for the technological manipulation of visual reality. Allen analogizes the way the mind perceives and deals with reality and the way the camera operates to record reality. In other words, Allen places the issue of the formation of individual personality and character in the context of the perception and construction of reality through the media. As in *Annie Hall* and *Manhattan*, in *Zelig* the social and cultural operations of the

74

camera and media relate to the dynamic structure and development of the individual psyche. Raising the question of appearance and reality through the vehicle of a mock documentary, a comedic form that immediately undermines any privileged perspective from which to document reality, the film also becomes a visual extension of internal psychic instability and uncertainty. The camera cannot provide the security the psyche craves. In an excellent scene of visual and verbal humor that fuses the different elements of the film together in an original and fascinating way, Zelig and Fletcher are in a therapy session. As a chameleon he naturally has been assuming the guise of a psychiatrist until she artfully turns the tables on him by lying and saying that she is not really a doctor. Now in agitated confusion, he gets physically ill, realizing he has to change from being a make-believe doctor to a patient. It is a funny and precious moment about the fragile barriers between sanity and health as well as the psychological perceptions of reality.

The scene works, of course, because of the developing relationship between Zelig and Fletcher. We know that Eudora really is the doctor with the degree and professional training. However, we also anticipate her love for Leonard that crosses over professional boundaries so that, in a sense, she ultimately shares his sickness with him. This serves to sustain the visual and thematic point about psychic sickness and reality. Sickness and cure tend to fuse, especially in a society of explosive fluidity and volatility. Thus, following his return from Munich and upside-down flight over the Atlantic with Eudora, Leonard tells the crowd of New Yorkers who honor him: "Right – I've never flown before in my life and it shows exactly what you can do if you're a total psychotic" (p. 125). Bellow says:

> The thing was paradoxical because what enabled him to perform this astounding feat was his (*Onscreen, looking at the offscreen interviewer*) ability to transform himself. Therefore his sickness was also at the root of his salvation and . . . (*Pauses*) I think it's interesting to view the thing that way, that it, it was his . . . it was his very disorder that made a hero of him. (p. 126)

Taken to its social and political extreme, such instability leads, as already noted, to the force Allen dreads in so many of his films, fascism. However, through the Fletcher–Zelig love affair, Allen emphasizes individual psychology and personal relationships as a counterforce to fascism, while associating the psyche with the operations and manipulations of the media.

It seems to me, therefore, that, in *Zelig*, Allen does for the technology of media what Chaplin achieved in his depiction of assembly-line industrialism in *Modern Times,* in which all of the mechanical and technological forces of conformity, artificiality, and cultural reproduction are arrayed against the individual to manipulate and subvert him. Chaplin ingeniously displays these forces, which ultimately reached their most destructive potential in his portrayals of Hitler in *The Great Dictator* and the lady killer in *Monsieur Verdoux.* In *Modern Times,* Chaplin turns such forces of conformity and artificial existence into art. The tramp enters the belly of the whale of the modern industrial establishment, which ingests him into the internal workings of its vast machinery. He becomes physically and psychologically connected to the assembly line. At the same time, in his artistry Chaplin converts oppression into artistic expression and renewal. He dominates and exploits the cruelty of the industrial system by making the process funny. As a result, he also makes a statement about the power of art to revolutionize the environment and of the individual spirit as embodied by the tramp to survive under terribly oppressive circumstances.

Similarly, in his own way, Allen in *Zelig* challenges our modern times through his rendering of the interaction of art and propaganda with psychoanalysis and sociology. The photographic image and the cinematic process, including its entire network of publicity and distribution – as dramatized by the use of footage of William Randolph Hearst at San Simeon with early Hollywood celebrities – also absorb and consume the individual, undermining personal identity and manipulating needs and desires. The process of *Zelig*'s artistry and technology testifies to the power of the media, not just to reflect or distort reality, but also to create a new environment of mediated reality for the individual and the mass audience. Media for Allen, as already noted, can function this way partly because of the mind's vulnerability to the photographic image. At the same time, Allen's film performs a similar function for our era that Chaplin's *Modern Times* and *The Great Dictator* achieved for people a half-century ago. It both exposes and transforms and thereby offers a promise of regeneration in spite of its somber message about the social and economic powers that affect us. Working through these issues artistically and intellectually, *Zelig* provides an introduction to *The Purple Rose of Cairo* in which the complex relationship between art and reality invades a movie theater in New Jersey and changes peoples lives.

Zelig works so well partly because its humor undermines our complacency about photographic and documentary reality. We do not usually think of photographic images and films as edited reality. We tend to consider them to be pure images or specific pieces of reality locked into a frame with internal balances of color and space. *Zelig,* of course, explodes this notion, but the humor perhaps constrains the potential level of insecurity the movie could engender. As we saw, Allen's humor in *Zelig* disarms even Hitler. To some of Allen's critics, this use of humor to cap off the volatility of the tensions within his films constitutes a major deficiency not just in *Zelig*, but in the Allen canon in general since he turned from making primarily zany comedies. Such critics feel that Allen's humor palliates the uncertainity and stress in his works and circumvents the truth of his artistic and social vision of the despair and anguish in the human condition. It seems to me, however, that Allen's humor, as demonstrated so frequently throughout such films as *Play It Again, Sam, Annie Hall,* and *Manhattan,* generally underscores his vision and actually gives a cutting edge to it by particularizing and humanizing his rendition of experience.

The Purple Rose of Cairo, I think, is another example of such a film. It becomes a very disturbing film in which the humor works to pursue important questions about fiction and reality that were raised in *Zelig.* In his *New York Times* interview, Allen spoke almost casually about the relationship between fantasy and reality in the film, laughing over the importance of ultimately choosing reality. In this interview, Allen uses the word "reality" the way Cecilia's husband, Monk, uses it when she leaves him, presumably to go to Hollywood with Gil Shepherd, the actor who plays the fictional character Tom Baxter who stepped out of the screen. Monk shouts, "Go, see what it is out there. (*Yelling, his hand at his mouth*) It ain't the movies! It's real life! It's real life, and you'll be back! You mark my words! You'll be back!"[6] For Monk, reality is simply obvious; it is out there, it's immediate, it's rough, it's life in New Jersey during the Great Depression when unemployment haunts every family and household. In fact, however, reality turns out to be far more difficult to understand than Monk imagines. Once Cecilia's perception of her world changes, reality also confounds Monk, although he learns nothing from the events that change his life.

In discussing precedents for Allen's treatment of reality and cinema, Canby, as we have seen, recalls Buñuel and Buster Keaton. The metaphor, of course, for the comparison between the world of acting and the world of reality goes much farther back, perhaps most famously to Shakespeare in *As You Like It* (II. vii. 139–40) and *Macbeth* (V. v.24–8). In Shakespeare the metaphor conveys the tragedy of our inability to grasp and control experience. The same applies to *The Purple Rose of Cairo.* The fact that the film remains funny in spite of the ultimate seriousness of its purpose only further suggests Allen's achievement. Allen repeats his success in *Manhattan* of fusing both the humorous and dramatically serious aspects of the film into an artistic whole. Furthermore, besides synthesizing comedy and tragedy, Allen, as Brode says, also makes one film out of "worlds" that are technically and visually distinct:

> Woody's thematic maturity is countered by a parallel growth in technical accomplishment. Working with Gordon Willis, he created two unique and separate visual "worlds" here: the b & w of the movie-within-the-movie ("*The Purple Rose*" exists midway between mimicry and nostalgia, a loving satire on thirties styles) and a carefully controlled color scheme for the movie itself.[7]

Indeed, the parallel development of two worlds and two stories structures the entire film. The major achievement in *The Purple Rose of Cairo*, however, involves Allen's establishment of the relationship between these two worlds and his engagement with such substantive issues as media, fiction, and reality. In the two parallel worlds of the film, we first should examine the world of Cecilia's everyday existence in the depression era. Cecilia's story in this world leaves little room for anything besides pathos, loneliness, and despair. On a psychological level, one would have to compare her existence to that of Eve, played by Geraldine Page in *Interiors,* who finds her marriage and her creative life finished at middle age. The dark mood of Cecilia's empty life also compares to the situations Allen dramatizes in later films such as *Another Woman* and *September,* both of which contain none of the humor that infuses *Annie Hall, Manhattan, The Purple Rose of Cairo, Hannah and Her Sisters,* and *Crimes and Misdemeanors.* Cecilia also lacks the sophistication and education of the characters in these other movies since both naïveté and vulnerability are essential aspects of her character and requirements for the plot.

Cecilia's everyday world extends directly into the second world of *The Purple Rose of Cairo,* the film within the film that plays in a local theater that Cecilia compulsively patronizes. In our first meeting with Cecilia, we understand that her love of the movies involves more than merely being a supportive fan. She is an addict, using Hollywood as a substitute for her miserable life. In this first scene, the theater manager talks to Cecilia on a first-name, personal basis, informing her of the impending arrival of a new movie, which turns out to be "*The Purple Rose of Cairo.*" "You're gonna like this one. It's better than last week, more romantic" (p. 321). In the cut to the next scene, we find Cecila at work as a waitress with her sister in a local diner filled with the noise and clatter of abusive and rude customers. In conversation with her sister, Cecilia's intimate knowledge of the lives of the stars and of the details of their films clearly suggests a nearly pathological fixation on a world of escapist fantasy. The continuous stream of complaints thrown at her by her boss and the customers attests to her lack of concentration and her inability to function.

Thus, when Tom Baxter, the romantic character in the interior movie, leaves the film to meet Cecilia, who has watched the film for at least five continuous showings after being fired from her job at the diner, we have been psychologically prepared for the startling event. The utterly impossible act of a character leaving the screen to talk to an infatuated fan already has psychological validity and artistic coherence. The fantastic world of the interior film already has been internalized in Cecilia's mind. The parallel stories are both Cecilia's. While this seems rather obvious, the brilliant visualizations of both worlds, what so many critics see as Allen's technical skill, may overshadow the importance of this narrative device. We need to remember, therefore, that the carefully designed narrative structure of the film, which includes the psychological basis of Cecilia's character, sustains and develops the visual joke. The fantasy on the screen resonates in Cecilia's mind, and it is Cecilia who brings the fantasy to life, not Tom Baxter. Through Tom's antics, we see Cecilia reposition herself in her environment in an attempt to gain a new understanding of herself.

Superficially, the events of the parallel worlds of fantasy and reality are so thoroughly separate and different that, on reflection, the film seems in danger of dissolution. However, Allen sustains the tension and the relationship between these radically divergent worlds by creating a discourse between them that forms a unified film. Monk is a major factor in bringing these worlds together. Cecilia's marriage to Monk, even more than her plight at the diner or her economic situation in the midst of the Depression, sets the stage for our acceptance of the world of the living interior film. Partly owing to the marvelous performance of Danny Aiello, the character of Monk is an extraordinarily successful achievement for Allen. He also represents an interesting variation in Allen's use of language in film. Nearly every word Monk utters has impact and force. There are few of the gaps and stutters that constitute the speech of other Allen characters. No speech impediments mitigate his aggressive dominance. Also, not just his speech, but his very presence on the screen emanates power. Every scene involving him has dramatic validity. Embodying the reality that Cecilia wishes to escape, he seems to become part of the urban landscape that helps to determine their lives. The fact that he also happens to be a totally negative force, one of Allen's most unredeemable characters, actually adds to his credibility. In addition, the violence at the core of his nature operates as a continual threat. The violence either becomes manifest or seethes just below the surface,

79

creating a tension of its own in his dealing with Cecilia. At the same time, he never becomes a stereotype or cartoon figure like the Mafia figures in *Broadway Danny Rose*. The combination of dialogue and drama always rings true. Psychologically, he makes Cecilia's turn to fantasy both believable and understandable. He could not be better as a foil to earn our sympathy for his perennial victim, his wife. The epitome of a street bully, he is the perfect heavy.

Furthermore, each scene with Monk contains a nuance in the form of a gesture, action, or dialogue that makes it special. We first meet him pitching pennies on the street, his apparent daytime activity to fill the hours made vacant by unemployment. His friends alert him to Cecilia's arrival. Part of his strength as a character comes from his prolonged adolescence, his treatment of Cecilia as a mother to satisfy his bullying demands: "Boy, am I glad to see you. You got any dough?" (p. 325). When she questions him, he reacts with a childlike defensiveness. He denies that jobs are available at the ice factory: "No, there's nothin'. I was there" (p. 325). She doesn't seem to believe him. "Yeah, I was there. All right?" he claims. He calls a woman, who has told Cecilia that the men only "make passes at the girls who walk by," a "douche bag" (p. 326). In spite of their poverty, he feels obliged to entertain his friends and have them "over tonight." His next line beautifully dramatizes his penchant for selfish rationalization: "Well, I got to get even, don't I? I owe everybody in town" (p. 326). When she persists, he plays on her guilt like a child: "Well, what do you want? Did I close the factory," he says, adding, "You think I like scratching around for work? (*Looking around*) Livin' like a bum the last two years?" (p. 327). The defensiveness reverts back to masculine aggression when he rejects her offer to go with her to the movies: "Cecilia you like sitting through that junk, okay? I'm gonna shoot crap, okay?" (p. 327). His implied separation of the world of men and women is simple and quite appropriate for the scene. All his ploys and emotions come together in his parting gestures and words of both violence and childish demand: "Hey, look, you're not my boss. And don't give me that look" (p. 328). He then says, "Come on, give us a hug, just one, come on" (p. 328). Patting her back condescendingly, he adds a final patronizing remark: "And don't come home late....I worry. All right?" (p. 328). As he turns to rejoin his friends, the action is again right on the mark. Free from his wife, but with her money in his pocket, he almost jumps with a sense of adolescent freedom, claps his hands, and shouts to his friends, "Let's go," the neighborhood bully happy to be back with his gang to pitch pennies and shoot crap (p. 328).

That evening Cecilia comes home from the movies to find him with another woman, Olga. Again, the pattern of speech and the physical action are perfect. Leaving with Olga, he says of Cecilia, "She's my ball and chain, or she tries to be" (p. 339), but when he returns to the apartment to find Cecilia packing to leave, Monk becomes the dissembler and whiner. First, he praises her meat loaf: "That, uh, stuff you made yesterday was delicious" (p. 340). Seeing her with her bags, he plays innocent, saying, "What's going on?" and then tries to belittle and humiliate her: "What? Because of before? . . . Because of Olga, is that it? Because that would be funny. That would be ridiculous. (*Laughing*) I mean, if it's because of Olga, you'd be making a bigger fool out of yourself than you usually are" (p. 340). When she persists, he whines again: "You can't leave. I need you. And, and you know I love you. Now look, I made a mistake" (p. 341). Underlying the brutishness of Monk's speech and physical manner, Aiello conveys a complexity of emotions and motives, a mixture of fear, anger, and confusion that contributes to his violent unpredictability. In the rest of the scene with Farrow, he goes through his entire repertoire of bullying and excuses to persuade her to stay, beginning with his explanation for how he settles disagreements: "Look, I hit you when you get out of line, and I never just hit you, I always warn you first and then if you don't shape up you get whacked." When that fails to convince her, he begins to lose patience: "Now listen, Cecilia. I don't know who's fillin' your head full of these crazy notions, but I've had enough" (p. 342). Then he demands more meat loaf and blames the whiskey: "Look, I'm sorry. I mean, I'm really sorry. Can't I be sorry? I drink, I get crazy. It's not me, it's the whiskey." In the midst of his barrage, he even interjects a word of truth without realizing its implications: "I'm like a little kid when it comes to you" (p. 342). When she finally leaves, he believes she will return, not out of love, but because there is no place else to go, as she soon discovers on the street where she encounters prostitutes working a neighborhood bar.

In another scene, Aiello rises from the table with a gesture of impending violence that has the power of a blow. This occurs when she returns to the apartment following her afternoon with Tom. This time Monk is eating voraciously and complaining, "There's too much pepper in the sauce. I told you to go easy on the pepper" (p. 368). He then explains that he won't be going out because "my back is acting up again. (*Burps*) You gotta give me one of your special rubdowns. I bought liniment" (p. 368). Planning a secret rendezvous with Tom, she stutters that she cannot immediately minister the massage. Aiello's pause is electric as his entire body signals the incipient outburst. Every gesture and move anticipate physical violence, as he walks toward her: "What do you mean, you can't" (p. 369). Cecilia breaks into a stream of stutters, searching her mind for an excuse to explain leaving the apartment that night. "You made plans?" he says (p. 369). Aiello's control makes his physical domination of the scene and his intimidation of her especially impressive and disturbing. At last she conceives of the lie of a baby-sitting job that night. Monk looks down in judgment of her, observing her nervousness, seemingly poised between a blow or a verbal assault. Cecilia's relief is palpable when he consents to the idea of letting her work that night "because we can use every penny" (p. 369). Later that night when she returns empty-handed, Monk explodes: "Cecilia, I told you to get paid, uh, in cash, didn't I?" (p. 391). He adds, "Yeah, yeah, sure. Leave something to you, you can bet you're going to get fouled up" (p. 391).

With Monk as her handle onto reality, Cecilia turns to the movies for a little adventure and romance. To retain Allen's term "fantasy" for this aspect of the film risks misunderstanding his true accomplishment, which involves more than a charming and nostalgic return to the times and movies of the Depression-era thirties. The word invites confusing the film with the kind of delightful make-believe of *The Wizard of Oz* or the common tactic of using dreams to suggest the world of the imagination. In fact, Cecilia's interaction with the world and story of *"The Purple Rose of Cairo,"* including her disruption of the narrative through her influence on Tom's decision to leave the screen, really entails a witty, humorous, and perceptive discourse on the relationship of fiction and reality.

When Tom steps out of the film and fulfills the potential of all art to enter directly into the lives of its audience, he disturbs and endangers the worlds on both sides of the screen. Naturally, everything in the film turns to chaos – narrative, dialogue, relationships. The characters are forced to deal with a new reality. They must reinvent themselves and find a purpose to their existence. Of course, the situation is clearly impossible. A film is not real life. If, however, real life can be seen or understood as a kind of film, a stage of light and movement, with players attempting with varying degrees of success and failure to handle their lines, then reality can be interpreted as mediated by language and narrative, in this case a language based on film itself. Thus, Henry, the interior film's creative spirit and *"sophisticated playboy/writer,"* considers the possibility that the whole situation "is merely a matter of semantics." He says, "Let's, let's just readjust our definitions. Let's redefine ourselves as the real world (*Pointing towards the offscreen theater*) and them as the world of illusion and shadow. You see, we're reality, they're a dream" (p. 437). Of course, like any normal person, the Countess, one of the leading characters in the interior film, naturally dismisses the idea as ridiculous: "You better calm down. You've been up on the screen flickering too long" (p. 438).

The Countess's agitation can be taken as a symptom of poststructural anxiety. The Countess could not possibly know it, but Henry's comment and theory relate to the work of Stanley Fish and other students of the antifoundational relationship between language and reality. Henry's insight and the film's elaborate development of the contrast and relationship between the two worlds of the screen and daily life suggest that the film shares an interest with much of contemporary criticism in the importance of language, symbolization, and interpretation as the inevitable means for understanding and dealing with all experience. Usually unconcerned about life on the "real" side of the screen, Henry suddenly finds that Tom's actions force him to think differently for a moment and consider the possibility that screens of language and interpretation both shield and create access to all reality. In terms of current critical concerns, Henry acquires a new insight into the absence of absolutes and the mutability of foundations of truth and reality. For example, Fish denies the existence of points of privileged insight into the interpretation of texts or experience and dispels the notion of the text as, in a famous, often-quoted phrase, a "privileged container of meaning."[8] This freedom places the task of interpretation on "interpretive communities" who must realize that all such interpretation rests on experience and belief rather than some absolute source or form of truth. Readings and interpretations of literature and experience, therefore, become "cultural and contextual."[9] This argument by Fish and others, even in this abbreviated and simplified form, seems instructive as to the situation and premises of Allen's film. Cecilia's relationship with the world of the interior film becomes one of interpretation. It is not just that the worlds on opposing sides of the screen reverse themselves, but that both environments require forms of textual analysis. Scripts and screenplays change as do environments and contexts, but interpretation persists.

Accordingly, Allen makes the process of artistic construction and interpretation crucial to his film. While the film teases about the obvious distinction between reality and fantasy, it goes well beyond Monk's simplistic understanding of what the world means by real. Reality and fiction become part of the same process of the interpretation of experience through the mediation of visual and verbal expression. Significantly, this process also includes the idea of freedom as a matter of interpretation and context. Freedom cannot be separated from the act of writing and creating one's story or text of experience. This delineation in the film of language, interpretation, and freedom turns on two themes: the necessity of fictionalizing and contextualizing experience in order to gain access to it and the importance of distinguishing between texts that enslave and those that enhance the possibility of freedom. The fact that the film frequently achieves its greatest humor in the elaboration of these themes makes one wish Allen would write literary and cinematic criticism.

Thus, Gil Shepherd's confusion as an actor and person about fiction and reality condemns him to a kind of slavish stupidity. Comments by him and others suggest a muddled bewilderment about the distinction between the realms of reality and fiction without indicating an appreciation for their complex interrelationship. When Shepherd learns that his character Tom has escaped from the screen, he bemoans the waste of his own creative energies: "Oh, my God! There g – I mean, you know, I worked so hard to make him real" and his agent responds, "Yeah, well, maybe you overdid it" (p. 382). As though responding to Gil, a studio press agent in a different scene complains, "The real ones want their lives fiction, and the fictional ones want their lives real" (p. 395), not realizing that both modes are dependent on each other.

The humor in these and other jokes about fiction and reality brilliantly straddles the line between the utter silliness of the situation and the ultimate complexity of the issue. At the core of the joke is the paradox of uncertainty about reality and our dependence upon others of equal ignorance and helplessness to participate in a process of truth seeking. So when Gil tells Cecilia that "I created him," she corrects him, "Well, didn't the man who wrote the movie do that?" and he feels compelled to concede, "Yes technically. But I made him live. I fleshed him out" (p. 399). Later he says of Tom, "My own creation plagues me" (p. 435). Confronting that plague in another argument, he accuses Tom of being "fictional" and appeals to Cecilia: "Tell him you *can't* love him. He's (*Laughing*) fictional! You want to waste your time with a fictional character? I mean, you're a sweet girl. You deserve an actual human" (p. 404). Saying that "Tom's perfect!" Cecilia attempts to articulate her dilemma over choosing between Tom and Gil, but Gil continues his effort to convince her that Tom "can't learn to be real. It's like learning to be a midget. It's not a thing you can learn. Some of us are real, some are not" (p. 404). As a narcissistic actor insensitive to deeper nuances of writing, Gil always misses the point about the complexity of fiction and the text. Cecilia, on the other hand, understands how fiction always compromises with reality. She says, "I – I – I just met a wonderful new man. He's fictional, but you can't have everything" (p. 434). Finally convinced to choose the actor, both by her deeper doubts and by some "*Purple Rose of Cairo*" movie characters, Cecilia forgets her own understanding of the necessity of fiction to shape reality. She explains to Tom, "See, I'm a real person. No matter how... how tempted I am, I have to choose the real world" (p. 459). Ironically, the real world to Gil the actor is Hollywood, the epitome of the unreal. "Come away with me to Hollywood!" he tells Cecilia (p. 457).

In terms of Allen's artistic creed and the direction of his entire career, Hollywood equates to Tom's return to the screen and the denial of the full artistic potential of film to create a new reality through the creative imagination. The Hollywood that produces such imitations of the brilliant Cole Porter as "*The Purple Rose of Cairo*" confines the imagination and intellect, although it also has the capacity for its own kind of genius in films like the Fred Astaire and Ginger Rogers movie *Top Hat* that closes the film. In essence, a decision about a text constitutes a decision about life and freedom, an idea that Gil finds incomprehensible. However, many of the other characters talk of wishing to be free from their scripts in order to find new ones. Tom says, "I want to live. I want to be free to make my own choices" (p. 363). Larry, played by Van Johnson, asks, "I wonder what it's like out there?" (p. 366) and then impulsively decides to try for it, saying, "I want to go too. I want to be free! I want out!" and is reprimanded by none other than Raoul Hirsch, the producer: "I'm warning you, that's Communist talk" (p. 393).

A "real" fictional communist in the interior "*Purple Rose of Cairo*" makes one of the film's funniest points about the script and freedom. The communist calls upon the other characters in the movie to act: "I don't want to sit around and wait. That's exactly what they want" (p. 436). The other characters find him "tedious," but he persists. "Look at us!" he cries – interrupted by the overlapping voice of the Countess, who says, "Not again" – "Sitting around, slave to some stupid scenario" (p. 436). However, when Arturo, the maitre d' at the movie's Copacabana, realizes that a revolution has occurred and the scenario has in fact been overturned, his reaction epitomizes a new sense of freedom gained through the possibility of creating his own script. He asks, "Are we just chucking out the plot, sir?" (p. 449). When Tom tells him, "It's every man for himself!" he intensely says, "Then I don't have to seat people anymore. I can do what it is I've always wanted to do!" He turns to the band, shouts, "Hit it, boys!" and bursts into a wonderful tap dance that earns the laughter and applause of the entire nightclub (p. 449).

Reducing centuries of discussion about God, determinism, and the meaning of life to a series of beautifully timed and executed lines, Allen highlights his theme of freedom and the writer by developing Flaubert's famous comparison of the writer to God who is felt everywhere but never seen. Cecilia takes Tom to a church, shows him a crucifix, and tries to explain the concept of God to him. He confuses the idea with his own sense of creation: "Oh, I think I know what you mean – the two men who wrote, – uh, *The Purple Rose of Cairo*. (*Gesturing, looking at the altar*) Irving Sachs and R. H. Levine, the writers who collaborate on films" (p. 408). Cecilia corrects him, making his point. She says, "I'm talking about something much bigger than that. No, think for a minute. (*Gesturing*) A reason for everything. Eh, otherwise, i – i – it – it'd be like a movie with no point, and no happy ending" (p. 408). The writer and God determine meaning through the power of narrative to create and structure the beginning, middle, and the end of the story. Later in his first visit to a whorehouse, Tom confesses his preoccupation with "some very deep things" and reveals that his thoughts are "about God and his relation with Irving Sachs and R. H. Levine" (p. 424).

While the humor and parody are apparent, the film's point about the connection between freedom and creative textual interpretation remains important. Indeed, the film plays with the viewer's sensibility when it puts an interesting twist on authorial and interpretive responsibility for the moral implications of narration. After being rejected by Cecilia in favor of Gil, Tom returns to the interior film to the great relief of all the characters, who speak lines indicating their happiness over the conclusion of the crisis and their expectation that things will return to normal. Unknown to them, their fate has been sealed. The real god of Hollywood, Raoul Hirsch the producer, and his entourage have decided to destroy the movie to prevent any future escapes. Eagerly expecting a future of exactly what they have experienced in the past, the characters of "*The Purple Rose of Cairo*" face the apocalypse at the hands of a chagrined god worried about lawsuits and complications. The studio will turn off the projector and burn the prints and the negative (p. 439). Again, Allen offers a joke that cuts like a knife. He declines to draw our attention to this impending disaster, preferring to concentrate on Cecilia's plight in her world instead. He simply lets us remember the prospective catastrophe as the characters cheerfully head toward oblivion. Allen's way of resolving the extended joke about the escaped character dramatizes the deeper point regarding the moral dimension of narrative that must include responsibility for endings. Unable to participate in the writing of their own stories, the characters are fated to either slavery or destruction.

Unhappily, a similar fate in the form of a miserable ending of loneliness awaits Cecilia, who seems to be denied the opportunity of choosing that was granted the *"Purple"* movie character Tom. "The most human of all attributes is your ability to choose," Larry tells her (p. 456). Gil, of course, runs off to Hollywood, leaving her standing not at the altar, but at the movie marquee. Moreover, Allen also does not give her the same chance granted Allan Felix in *Play It Again, Sam* to reinvent and reconstruct herself at the movies. We have seen her as a terrible victim, but we also have recognized vivaciousness, intelligence, and charm in her. Ironically, it strains credibility to see her return to the Jewel Theater only to smile and lose herself in *Top Hat* without having learned from her own fictional experience with reality. The end leaves her without creative choices, but we have seen her make and act upon choices throughout the film. Apparently, the end is designed to contain the film's humor by insisting upon the seriousness of her situation as the victim of Monk and the economic and social conditions of the times. Her inner life will continue to be at the movies, presumably in imitation of those millions who actually suffered such a fate during the Depression.

However, by choosing this ending for *The Purple Rose of Cairo* rather than the happy ending of *Zelig*, Allen sacrifices her freedom so as to impose freedom of interpretation on the viewer. Similarly, by typecasting the black maid, Delilah, he imposes on the audience the need to consider her place and position in the movie, in relation to the characters not only in the interior film, but also in the world of the 1930s. Thus, Lloyd Rose misses the deeper point when he seems to condemn Allen for making films that disturb his public because "the audience didn't know what to think" about them.[10] If nothing else, Allen obviously hopes to force his audience to think for itself. In *The Purple Rose of Cairo,* he teases about the audience that balks over such a requirement. One woman complains, "I want what happened in the movie last week to happen this week, otherwise what's life all about anyway" (p. 373). Similarly, Tom objects to the distress involved in thinking about life: "Look, I'd – I don't want to talk any more about what – what's real and what's illusion. Life's too short to spend time thinking about life. Let's just live it" (p. 440). Clearly, Allen hopes *The Purple Rose of Cairo* will evoke interpretation from its audience as well as laughs. Indeed, his awareness of these issues of media, reality, and freedom seems apparent in his comments to Eric Lax. According to Lax, "He feels that *The Purple Rose of Cairo* is the best film he's made, and that *Zelig* ranks as one of his better efforts."[11] Obviously pleased with the result of his efforts in *The Purple Rose of Cairo* and *Zelig*, Allen, I believe, surpasses his achievements in these films in two subsequent movies, *Hannah and Her Sisters* and *Crimes and Misdemean-*

ors, films that compensate for less successful efforts during these years such as *Another Woman* and *September.*

Notes

1. Eric Lax, "Woody Allen – Not Only a Comic," *New York Times,* Sunday, February 24, 1985, Section 2, pp. 1, 24.

2. Vincent Canby, "Screen: Woody Allen's New Comedy, *Purple Rose of Cairo,*" *New York Times,* March 1, 1985, p. C8; and Canby, "Film View: Woody Allen Journeys From Page to Screen," *Sunday New York Times,* March 17, 1985, Section 2, pp. 19, 26.

3. Graham McCann, *Woody Allen: New York* (Cambridge: Polity, 1990), pp. 181, 182.

4. See Douglas Brode, *Woody Allen: His Films and Career,* 2nd. ed. (Secaucus, N.J.: Citadel, 1987), p. 228.

5. Woody Allen, *Zelig* in *Three Films of Woody Allen* (New York: Vintage, 1987), p. 67. Subsequent references to this film will be to this edition and will be included parenthetically in the text.

6. Woody Allen, *The Purple Rose of Cairo* in *Three Films of Woody Allen* (New York: Vintage, 1987), p. 464. All subsequent references to this film will be to this edition and will be quoted parenthetically in the text.

7. Brode, p. 251.

8. Stanley Fish, *Is There a Text in this Class? The Authority of Interpretive Communities* (Cambridge, Mass.: Harvard University Press, 1980), p. 3.

9. Stanley Fish, *Doing What Comes Naturally: Change, Rhetoric, and the Practice of Theory in Literary and Legal Studies* (Durham, N.C.: Duke University Press, 1989), p. 29.

10. Lloyd Rose, "Humor and Nothingness," *Atlantic,* May 1985, p. 95.

11. Eric Lax, *Woody Allen: A Biography* (New York: Knopf, 1991), pp. 371–2.

5
Hannah and
Her Sisters

He doesn't appear on screen for many minutes, but everything has his name on it, including of course the black and white credits that acknowledge him as writer and director and actor. His signature appears everywhere else as well: the *"sultry"* trumpet of "You Made Me Love You" that opens the film and immediately breaks into *"an up tempo jazz number,"* the use of titles that no other director would try in quite that way, the voice-over as the first spoken words in the film, the perfect gag lines. And yet things are also different. *Hannah and Her Sisters* can be seen as a metaphor for the Woody Allen canon. It is the same and yet different, literally achieving a new plateau of artistic range and unity. A culmination of all his other work, *Hannah and Her Sisters* includes elements from most of Allen's major films – the comedic but creative schlemiel, the focus on serious women characters of *Interiors* and *Manhattan,* complex characterization and narrative, the exploration of ambiguous personal relationships and moral issues, the fusion of comedy and drama, self-conscious cinematography, and visualization; but it also represents a transformation. For those critics who see in Allen's work true milestones in the history of American cinema, *Hannah and Her Sisters* realizes the creative potential of all of his important films as well as the fulfillment of a promise about his artistic values and objectives that he has made throughout his mature years and repeated in his interview with Eric Lax for the *New York Times.*

Significantly, in this interview he discusses his aesthetic criteria and objectives in terms of his desire to be original and to venture into new areas:

I've tried to mix my films up very deliberately with *Interiors* and *A Midsummer Night's Sex Comedy* and *Stardust Memories* and *Zelig,* and be in most of them, and do funny ones and more serious ones, and black and white ones, and color ones. My hope would be to keep fresh.

The wish to be "fresh," however, runs into the expectations of audiences that are repelled, like the audience in *The Purple Rose of Cairo,* by the unexpected and unconventional:

It's a tough thing. People perceived early on in my career that I was able to make funny movies that would make them laugh. They always feel someway suspicious or wondering what my motives are if I don't do it. One of the problems that I'm skirting is that for me, the easiest kind of film to do is the knock-down, drag-out comic film. It's no big deal, it's just the thing that comes most naturally to me. But I'm trying to do things that are much more difficult for me and that I have to stretch for and risk doing a miserable picture.

The internal pressure Allen feels to strive for such new forms of creative expression anticipates the wishes of some in his audience, while at the same time encountering an almost physical resistance from others. As he told Lax:

I always try to do films that have humor in them, but also have other things going for them, like interesting stories or some dimension or something of value that will stick to people's ribs in a different way. But each time you do that you run the risk of alienating part of your audience. And I do alienate them a certain amount of the time. They do come in sometimes and say, "Well, gee, yes, I guess it was pretty, and it was this, but it wasn't very funny." I would want to stop them all and say, "Yes, I know it's not as funny as *Love and Death,* but forget that I did it and see if you like it for what it is." And, I don't know, they might grab me back by the lapels and say, "We don't!" But that's what I'm trying to do.[1]

And yet it should be noted that for skeptics of Allen's originality, all of the presumably fresh elements and concepts that are said to comprise his work are largely derivative, "Xeroxed" borrowings. To his detractors, Allen merely repackages and markets the breakthroughs of his many predecessors from Welles to Bergman whom Allen himself recognizes and acknowledges. To his admirers, however, Allen, like innovators in any field or art, uses and transforms the work of others to create original art with his own signature. Such Allen partisans point to the opening of *Hannah and Her Sisters* as a testimony to his originality.

Figure 3. "God, she's beautiful" is how Elliot, played by Michael Caine, sees Barbara Hershey as Lee, the youngest of the three sisters in the opening shot of *Hannah and Her Sisters*. (Orion)

Indeed, the first scene immediately establishes a new intensity of compactness and concreteness for Allen, the very stylistic qualities that Walter Blair cites as crucial in the development of another American genius of humor, Mark Twain.[2] The scene also warrants some extended commentary because of its importance to the structure and development of the rest of the film. The opening seconds of the film concentrate on the full-face shot of Lee, Hannah's beautiful younger sister, played by Barbara Hershey (Fig. 3). The shot takes in her half-smile and gaze, conveying the irresistible combination of youthfulness and precocity that made Mariel Hemingway's portrayal of Tracy so powerful in *Manhattan*. The shot visually confirms what the black and white title on the screen already has told us, "God she's beautiful."[3] Allen then uses the technique of the voice-over to take us directly into the interior consciousness of the character looking at her – Elliot, played by Michael Caine. In a long single take that characterizes Allen's method and style throughout the film, the camera follows her as she circulates among the guests at the Thanksgiving Day party, thereby revealing the apartment setting and establishing the milieu, but also exhibiting in more detail her beauty and charm as she moves. With Elliot's voice-over describing his reactions and feelings, we are immediately in the midst of an intense dramatic situation that grows increasingly complicated by the conclusion of his monologue.

Moreover, the scene, especially with Elliot's narration, embodies the theme of the camera as a machine built on visual desire and sexual differentiation. However, the difference between this opening and Alvy's monologue in *Annie Hall* is significant. In the earlier film, Alvy basically tells us about narrative desire, whereas here the camera and the film not only show us such narrative desire, but place us right in the middle of it as participants. At the same time, the camera positions us in a way that at once aligns us with the male perspective, but also undermines that perspective as both the scene and the film develop.

In the intensity of the gaze that follows Lee on an expanding social field, Elliot's voice-over becomes a dramatic monologue of desire and doubt. He begins with the obsession of *Manhattan*, a woman's beauty: "She's got the prettiest eyes, and she looks so sexy in that sweater" (p. 5). He moves into fantasy and self-justification: "I just want to be alone with her and hold her and kiss her... and tell her how much I love her and take care of her" (p. 6). The next line immediately puts another twist to the situation and reveals Allen's pursuit of the difficult and complex in his exploration of human relationships. It also suggests Allen's continued interest in the theme of desire described earlier as the displaced and decentered wishes of the unconscious for sexual completion and personal fulfillment. When Elliot's self-doubt and guilt reveal that the object of his desire is his sister-in-law, Allen effectively intensifies the drama of desire in *Annie Hall* and *Manhattan* by moving it in *Hannah and Her Sisters* to the midst of the source of desire in the family. Also, Elliot's self-doubt turns his inner voice into a dialogue of doubts that adds to the complexity of the characterization and the drama. Elliot thinks, "Stop it, you idiot. She's your wife's sister. But I can't help it" (p. 6).

The monologue, however, continues to reveal the depth of Elliot's obsession and to indicate the impossibility of easy resolution:

I'm consumed by her. It's been months now. I dream about her. I –
I, think about her at the office. Oh, Lee. (*Sighing*) What am I going
to do?...I hear myself mooning over you, and it's disgusting. Before,

92

when she...squeezed past me in the doorway, and I smelled that perfume on the back of her neck...Jesus, I, I thought I was gonna swoon!

Elliot's last thought before the interruption of his voice-over by Hannah, his wife, who is played by Mia Farrow, concerns the danger his feelings present to his image and dignity: "You're a financial advisor. It doesn't look good for you to swoon" (pp. 6–7). To compound his guilt, when Elliot is startled from his reverie by Hannah, she instantly conveys her warmth and love by *"Rubbing his shoulder"* and calling him "Sweetheart" (p. 7).

Elliot's visual pursuit of Lee around the apartment has revealed an atmosphere of affluence and sophistication. The decor of the apartment as well as the dress and body language of the guests at the party all suggest comfort, conviviality, and a degree of privilege. As the camera and film move from Elliot's consciousness and desire to Hannah and the others celebrating Thanksgiving together, Allen's direction and script sustain the intensity of the opening moments of the scene. Precisely such intensity is suggested with the entrance from a hallway of Hannah's sister, Holly, who is played by Dianne Wiest. She seems to introduce an alien or disruptive element into the festive Thanksgiving atmosphere. As in *Manhattan,* Allen here also carefully constructs his interior spaces to create significant visualizations. The hallway through which Holly enters is angular and visually jarring. It fragments and breaks up what previously had been a scene of connection and continuous movement. As she enters, Hannah and Elliot go off-screen, at least visually abandoning Holly, who holds a tray of hors d'oeuvres and eats and swallows with apparent self-conscious discomfort. When she speaks, *"Holding her hand to her mouth,"* her body language indicates a kind of guilty, nervous insecurity. The scene then cuts to Hannah's kitchen where Holly soon reveals the source of her insecurity.

In the kitchen, Allen switches gears, so to speak. Instead of continuing to emphasize visualizations to develop the potential of the scene, he turns to humor, dialogue, and the effective acting of Farrow and Wiest. Here, Allen maturely contextualizes his humor within a world of tensions, relationships, and characterizations, thereby advancing his technique of fusing drama and comedy that was so celebrated in *Annie Hall* and *Manhattan.* Also, in this scene a special delicacy and subtlety in both the direction and action manifest themselves. As the action in the kitchen progresses, small, subtle gestures and expressions achieve a fresh significance and power, adding to the overall complexity of the scene and the levels of communication within it. Thus, the conversation in the kitchen provides considerable background to the sisters' relationships to each other, information that also will help explain the nature of their future relationships. We soon realize that Holly has been dependent financially on Hannah for some time and that she has been unable to establish a permanent career or even an identity for herself: "Hannah, I have to borrow some more money. . . . Don't get upset." Somewhat like a child, she promises that "this is the last time, I promise. And I'm keeping strict accounts" (p. 9). Hannah responds truthfully that she never gets upset over money and would be insulted over any undue concern about the issue. Indeed, if money were the matter, it would be a relatively easy situation to deal with for both Hannah and Holly. Instead, Allen develops dramatic intensity by making the issue be Hannah's maternal instincts as well as Holly's habitual insecurity and irresponsibility.

Accordingly, when Holly requests two thousand dollars, Hannah's body language and facial gestures communicate a definite surprise and hesitation. Nothing is said yet to convey the nature or reason behind Hannah's hesitation, but the feeling and the resulting tension, which already were anticipated by Holly's excessive nervousness, are palpable. Holly tries to explain how she will spend the money to establish a catering business, when Hannah interjects a question that immediately arouses our laughter because it responds to the nervous undercurrent of the scene, while clarifying Holly's problem in a way that is not completely unexpected. Also, the subject of the question and its swift exposure of Holly make it perfect for the dramatic and humorous effect that Allen wishes to create. Hannah asks, "Are we talking about cocaine again?" (p. 10). The question decisively reveals not only Holly's past drug dependence and overall unreliability, but also the judgmental and detached element in Hannah's character that Hannah fails to recognize fully in herself. The oldest and most responsible of the sisters, Hannah has been something of a surrogate mother figure for the others and continues to function with this edge of superiority over them. This aspect of her personality will grow more important in the movie as a source of estrangement for Hannah from her family and those she loves.

Wiest's portrayal of Holly's character is especially sensitive. Her actions and gestures evoke insecurity and embarrassment and dramatize her position within the family as a middle-aged, middle daughter who still has not found a place for herself. Her denial about drug use and her promises fuel her insecurity as they inevitably arouse suspicion: "I swear. I swear. We've already got some requests to do a few dinner parties" (p. 100). She then launches into a more detailed explanation about her future plans to advance her acting career, describing how she will combine both the new catering business at night with auditions and acting classes during the day. However, her explanations set us up to laugh over her last line, which shatters the pretense of her confidence: "I haven't done drugs in a year" (p. 11). Holly's defensive, yet funny comment has the double-edge of continued uncertainty regarding her situation in the present and her direction for the future.

At the same time, Hannah's tendency to impose her doubts and worries in a somewhat nagging way also manifests itself a few minutes later when she describes a man that she has in mind for Holly as "a lot better than your ex-husband. He's got a good job.... He's – he's – he's not a dope addict or anything." Still tense and awkward, Holly reacts, "Give me a break" (p. 15). Thus, in very brief interactions within a prolonged opening scene, Allen uses dialogue both humorously and dramatically to delineate these central characters and their history with each other. In conjunction with his presentation of Elliot's inner thoughts about Lee, Allen establishes a perfect pace for the beginning of this film. At the same time, he creates an important stylistic pattern for the film in that the dialogue, acting, and humor also operate somewhat indirectly. In other words, we see things – actions, gestures – and hear things – jokes, dialogue – that do not simply tell us what to think and see, but enable us to position ourselves within the film to engage in our own interpretation and to think for ourselves.

For example, there is the presentation in this opening scene of Hannah's parents, played magnificently by Lloyd Nolan as the father Evan and Farrow's real-life mother, Maureen O'Sullivan, as Norma. As background to the events of the evening, we hear Evan and Norma in Hannah's living room "floating down memory lane again" (p. 11), as Lee says. With the family and guests assembled all around them, Evan plays the piano and sings "Bewitched" with Norma to everyone's pleasure. They are a show business couple and the family expects them to entertain. And yet even here, Allen's inclination toward artistic complexity operates amid what appears to be rather apparent domestic simplicity and harmony. Allen positions the couple in a way that visually suggests their marginal relationship to their own family, a situation that gains significance as the film progresses. The visual and dramatic marginalization of Evan and Norma highlights their absence, their lack of central involvement in the midst of a family celebration for Thanksgiving. Hannah, not her mother, occupies the center of this family and keeps it together. The parents are decorative. They are more show than substance, both as people and parents. Subtly suggested in the opening scene, the exposure of the darker facts about her parents and her upbringing achieves fuller expression later in the film when Hannah races to her parents' apartment to help settle a fight between them that erupted, as Evan describes it, when:

95

We were making a commercial down at the mayor's office, and there was this young, good-looking salesman...and your mother was throwing herself at him in a disgusting way, and when she found she was too old to seduce him, that he was just embarrassed by her – ... Then at lunch she got drunker and drunker and finally she became Joan Collins. (p. 88)

Norma's denials, her charge that Evan is a "haircut that passes for a man" (p. 89) who never possessed any talent, reveals a history of fighting between them, including a series of infidelities. When Norma claims that only Hannah's talent enables them to survive financially, Evan responds, "I can only hope that she was mine. With you as her mother...her father could be anybody in Actor's Equity," and Norma readily agrees that "she's talented ...so it's not likely she's yours!" (p. 89).

As the fight subsides into the same kind of sentimental musical reverie that characterized the Thanksgiving evening, Hannah has time to reflect on her parents and their absence in her life. She thinks:

She was so beautiful at one time, and he was so dashing. Both of them just full of promise and hopes that never materialized. . . . And the fights and the constant infidelities to prove themselves...and blaming each other. It's s – sad. They loved the idea of having us kids, but raising us didn't interest them much. But it's impossible to hold it against them. They didn't know anything else. (pp. 90–1)

In this later scene, as Hannah ponders, the camera literally gives us Norma's and Evan's life together, revealing them *"beautiful, hopeful"* in family photographs that have the multiple effect of showing the real actors as they looked once, while also going back into Hannah's youth to suggest some source in early family unhappiness for her current life-style and her profound hopes for domestic security with Elliot and her children. The photographs provide further demonstration of Allen's innovation as a director even with minimal materials and props.

In the opening scene, the setting with Norma and Evan at the piano disguises the rivalry and anger that exists between them and entails a countermovement to the tensions that consistently crop up during the evening for the other characters. Thus, in the kitchen, Lee, Hannah, and Holly discuss Norma's drinking problems and her habitual flirtatiousness. However, when Lee leaves, Hannah and Holly discuss Lee's relationship with her "angry" and "depressive" older lover, Frederick. As some children depart, Holly confesses that "God, it gets so lonely on the holidays" (p. 14), a line that perfectly anticipates the entrance of her friend and catering partner, April, played by Carrie Fisher, who ultimately will contribute to her loneliness through her competition over men and work. April asks, "Am I interrupting... any sister talk?" (p. 15), a provocative line replete with ironies for its suggestion of a special intimacy between sisters, who contain in their intense mutual involvements all of the destructive potential that exists undisguisedly in the world outside of their family bond.

Fittingly, Hannah accidentally hurts and pricks Holly with a toothpick as Elliot and Lee meet alone in the bedroom. The developing attraction between Elliot and Lee remains barely below the surface. She describes a drawing of her that Frederick sold that week: "Yeah, it was, it was one of his better drawings, a very beautiful nude study. Actually, it was of me. (*Laughing*) It's funny, you know, it's a funny feeling to know you're being hung naked in some stranger's living room." After describing this drawing, she looks off-screen at Elliot, surprised but probably pleased over his reaction to her description of the drawing: "Well, you can't tell it's me, although – (*Pausing*) You're turning all red, Elliot" (p. 18). As Lee continues to describe her own uncertainties about work, career, and possible courses at Columbia University, Hannah enters to tell Lee, "You look so beautiful" (p. 19). "Doesn't she look pretty?" she says to both of them in apparent innocence. Lee's lines that follow this constitute the film's first reference to the character played by Woody Allen, Mickey Sachs. They are significantly overlapped by Elliot's agreement about Lee's beauty: "I bumped into your ...ex-husband on the street the other day.... He was, he's just as crazy as ever. He was on his way to get a blood test" (p. 19). Thus, Mickey enters the conversation as an alien character who still retains some relation to the group. Without yet meeting Mickey, we get the essence of his character in a way that is consistent with the film's compactness and intensity.

The structure of *Hannah and Her Sisters* sustains the power and momentum of the film's opening scene. In many ways, the structure of *Hannah and Her Sisters* compares to that of *Manhattan*.[4] Once again we see parallel love stories that interconnect by virtue of the affairs and yearnings of vagarious lovers. In this case, of course, the women are sisters, which adds an intensity and intimacy to their relationships. The bond of sisterhood gives them an inherent and important connection to each other, which the women in *Manhattan* really lacked. In essence, to establish this line of development, Allen simply extends in dramatic and temporal terms the relationships that already have been presented in the opening scene. The sisters' lives are indeed so close to each other that the narrative lines intertwine. They really cannot escape each other psychologically or emotionally. One of the beauties of the film is Allen's sensitivity to their dependence on one another even when hurting, deceiving, and undermining each other. There is a true sense of sisterly and family relationships in his presentation of these three women – four counting the effervescent and charming mother.

Furthermore, in telling the individual and collective stories of these four impressive female characters, Allen, it can be argued, finally has completed his *Manhattan* project of making a great movie about women. *Hannah and Her Sisters* is their movie in a way that *Manhattan* never quite becomes the possession of the women in it. With its detailed study of the inner and external lives of these women, *Hannah and Her Sisters* structures what has been his admitted life-long obsession with women. As Maureen Dowd in the *New York Times* says, Allen "revels in exploring the feelings, drives, problems and strengths of women." In her interview with Allen, which appeared upon the release of the film, Allen says, "I have a tremendous attraction to movies or plays or books that explore the psyches of women, particularly intelligent ones. When Mary McCarthy wrote *The Group*, I couldn't wait to get my hands on it, or the Richard Yates novel, *Easter Parade*." Allen goes on to say how he actually prefers to work with women and even identifies with them: "I very rarely think in terms of male characters, except for myself only." He told Dowd that he accounts for this fascination with women because of his upbringing: "I was the only male in a family of many, many women. I had a sister, female cousins, a mother with seven sisters. I was always surrounded by women."[5]

Mickey Sachs's story provides the comic undercurrent to the stories of the sisters. It weaves its way in and out of the narrative, offering wonderful comic relief, but also maintaining continuity throughout the film. As Hannah's first husband, he is part of the extended family, which gives him considerable access to the parallel relationships. Of course, Mickey's story is only one of several other male parallels to the women's stories, the others being Elliot's infatuation for Lee, which competes with Frederick's paternalistic relationship to her. In addition to developing these parallel narrative structures involving Mickey, Elliot, Frederick, and even Evan to some extent, Allen also creates unity and control over his material through several other brilliant techniques and motifs. The contrivance of titles as introductions to sequences of narrative works to great effect. The titles form narrative frames for different parts of the film and enable Allen to concentrate on the content of each of the sequences as though they are distinct dramatic entities that are still connected to the whole. Each narrative sequence contains its own world of action and character development. Also, as Graham McCann and others note, the sound track of the film forms another means of linking the sequences to each other and to the film as a whole. Different sequences and the characters within them have their own musical themes that play throughout the film, almost in the manner of silent movies, a similarity that seems especially appropriate when new titles on the screen are announced by new musical motifs. The music, therefore, proffers a method of continuity and development of both mood and tone as well as theme and characterization. The theme of Thanksgiving as a special family holiday also binds and structures the film. The film opens and closes with Thanksgiving celebrations that are three years apart, while a second celebration takes place in the middle of the film at a moment of crisis and uncertainty in the characters' lives. All of these elements make *Hannah and Her Sisters* one of Allen's most structured and compact films. The tightness of structure, in turn, helps to make the film especially powerful, moving, and believable.

With these many linkages between the series of parallel narratives, the most interesting involves the subtextual similarity between Mickey's search and the lives of the female characters. Seemingly different in so many ways, the story of Mickey in fact is the comic counterpart to their individual quests. He functions as a comic mirror image for their strife. Mickey's character becomes Allen's way of placing himself in the field of action without destroying the film as being primarily about their narrative of desire. It remains their story with Mickey providing comic relief and narrative energy. Thus, we should remember that we are first introduced to him only indirectly by Lee's reference to him as being as crazy as ever. Of course, his nervousness will only turn out to be different in kind from the problems the others face. Nevertheless, when we do first meet him, he functions in the midst of near madness as a producer of a television program suggestive of "Saturday Night Live" with its controversial and unconventional comedy sketches about the Pope and child molestation or President Reagan. Clearly, the tensions and demands of this job, with its excessively sensitive writers who won't tolerate any editorial revision of their work, performers who overdose on drugs moments before show time, and censorship officials from Standards and Practices, contribute to Mickey's inclination toward hypochondria. As in *Annie Hall, Zelig,* and other films, in this movie physical sickness generally signifies psychological dysfunction. Dragged and pulled by innumerable demands for the show's production, Mickey's cry for a Tagamet for his ulcer constitutes a call for psychological and spiritual help: "Christ, this show is ruining my health!" (p. 33). It also keeps him from visiting his children. When he does drop in on Hannah, it is with immediate excuses: "I got two minutes. 'Cause, God, the show is killing me. I got a million appointments today" (p. 33).

Mickey's hypochondria takes him to a specialist for whom he cannot quite remember which ear is experiencing deafness. The hypochondria is a great joke that becomes infinitely funnier when the doctor's diagnosis suggests the possibility of real illness. Although it keeps Mickey up at night and drives him to utter panic and distraction, it is impossible to take the idea of his illness seriously. The doctors force him to undergo all kinds of frightening examinations that require him to encounter and enter into monstrous-looking machines that resemble Chaplin's encounters in *Modern Times*. Foreign objects are plugged into his body in the attempt to locate serious illness. The victim of modern medicine and technology just as Chaplin's tramp and Allen's Zelig were victims of other forms of technology, Mickey becomes the epitome of the trapped alien. His medical prisons are mere extensions of the prisons of other aspects of his life. Placed in ridiculous and humiliating positions by his own hypochondria, Mickey stands for the self-imprisonment of all the other characters in the film as well. We observe him with laughter, but part of us also goes with him into those imposing machines of medical technology. Thus, we naturally also appreciate his jump for joy when he learns that a wrong diagnosis now leaves him in good health.

At this point, when the joke should be over, Allen puts a new twist on it. No longer able to substitute physical symptoms for his psychic unhappiness, Mickey's hypochondria doesn't disappear with his bodily health, but manifests itself instead in a kind of existential hypochondria. In other words, he invents a form of mental or philosophical illness that prevents him from truly examining the psychological roots of his unhappiness, which concern the absence in his life of love, not religion. Based on his sudden encounter with the possibility of his own death, the very idea of death in the absence of ultimate truth leads him to believe that life lacks all meaning. The silliness of his hypochondria becomes transformed into the absurdity of his existential quest for a conclusive and total meaning to life. He becomes thoroughly disillusioned and depressed, quitting his job and shirking any productive activity. In essence, the hypochondria simply assumes another form – this time an existential one – as a symptom of emotional and psychological needs. However, Mickey's pain becomes the viewer's pleasure as his search for the meaning of life takes us into some wonderful scenes: his exploration of Catholicism, his questioning of a Hare Krishna leader, his confrontation with his parents who find his rejection of Judaism and his questions about the meaning of life ridiculous, and his disillusionment with the failure of the great thinkers of the West such as Freud and Nietzsche.

All of these scenes – from Mickey's first medical examination to his search for religious truth – work so well because they are comedic counterparts to the narratives of desire. In his wanderings through the streets of New York, Mickey replicates the search for completeness and psychic unity that also motivates the other characters. In this way, his journey of jokes is thoroughly integrated into the rest of the film.

At the same time, the journey takes on a distinctive quality, not simply because of the humor, but also because Mickey, as the embodiment of everyone's alienation, goes alone. Mickey must search on his own for a means of fulfillment and happiness. In terms of the film's structure and process, Mickey's isolation finds visual and dramatic confirmation through the technique of flashbacks. Only Mickey experiences significant flashbacks, a form of internal communication and dialogue with one's self that occurs by reliving or imagining one's past. Like so much in this film, the flashbacks are dramatically significant, while also maintaining the movie's humor. In one case, Mickey recalls a medical problem that seemingly was not a product of hypochondria – infertility. The sequence of scenes that depicts this crisis in Hannah's and Mickey's life exemplifies how Allen's maturity occurs without a sacrifice of his ingenious capabilities as a comedic director and writer. Mickey and Hannah are told of his problem during a visit to Dr. Smith whose deadpan announcement of the situation coupled with his description of its potential impact on their marriage is classic Allen comedy at the expense of a dehumanized and insensitive medical profession. Dr. Smith says, "I realize this is a blow. My experience is that many fine marriages become unstable and are destroyed by an inability to deal with this sort of problem" (p. 69).

In the next scene, the camera follows Mickey and Hannah as they discuss the situation on Greenwich Village's Grove Street. They exchange some of the movie's funniest lines, all for the purpose of emphasizing his humiliation. Hannah asks, "Could you have ruined yourself somehow?" as a result, for example, of "excessive masturbation?" Allen responds, "Hey, you gonna start knocking my hobbies? Jesus!" (p. 69). When Hannah indicates that she prefers artificial insemination to adoption in order to "experience childbirth," he says, "You want a – a defrosted kid? Is that your idea?" (p. 70).

Both scenes with the doctor and with Hannah provide a setup for one of Allen's most masterfully executed comic moments in which Mickey and Hannah tell their best friends, Norman and Carol, played by Tony Roberts and Joanna Gleason, that they want Norman to be the sperm donor. The timing, dramatic action, and camera work are perfect. Hannah tentatively starts to introduce the subject, "We – we

...we had something we – we really wanted to discuss with you," but Mickey immediately takes over, gesturing and pacing nervously. The viewer knows the situation; Norman and Carol do not. The camera closes in on their faces as Mickey proceeds to explain. Their facial expressions and exchange of glances are marvelous. We read the scene on their faces, which anticipate Mickey's spoken lines as the situation grows clearer to them. Mickey says, "Right. We felt that if we were gonna do it, that we would like somebody who we knew and who we liked and who was warm and bright and..." (p. 73). He then further explains, "Yeah, well, I would be the father. (*Pointing to Norman*) You would just have to masturbate into a little cup," to which Norman, affecting a wonderful insouciance, responds, "I can handle that" (p. 73). When Hannah then adds nervously, "Obviously we wou – wouldn't have intercourse" (p. 73), Carol breaks up, finally verbally expressing the consternation and anxiety that have been appearing steadily on her face.

Mickey's infertility symbolizes his alienation from the human community and his lonely internal division. As recalled through another flashback, his attempts to find companionship and love include a date with Holly, an evening that becomes most notable for their bickering and arguing over drugs, music, and manners. Their evening together serves to reinforce the relevance of Mickey's symbolism as the solitary man for the rest of the characters. At the time of their date, Mickey and Holly occupy separate spaces of such loneliness and uncertainty that only miscommunication and assault are possible. The depth of Holly's fear and loneliness matches Mickey's. Her situation is expressed with sensitivity when she sits in the back of a car as David, a man she likes (played by Sam Waterston), drives with April, who is sitting next to him in the front of the car. Her position in the car graphically dramatizes her sense of isolation and despair. A shot from Holly's point of view illustrates her alienation, especially as it catches April leaning intimately toward David to speak to him. Holly's ruminations are expressed through her voice-over, but every word is visible on her face. Every emotion, feeling, and conflict is registered there. It is a brilliant moment of acting and direction, another consummation of old techniques applied in a new way that comprise the details and specifics of this film (pp. 55–6).

In developing his parallel stories, Allen offsets Holly's pathos and desperation and Mickey's isolation with Elliot's foolish infatuation and Frederick's pomposity. Depicting Elliot as clumsy and awkward, Allen relies on considerable physical action to develop his character in a way that exaggerates these weaknesses in him. The street scenes between Elliot and Lee come off with comedic brilliance as he races madly to effect an accidental encounter with her or to call her from a pay phone after impetuously and disastrously kissing her in the loft studio she shares with Frederick. The obvious ploy of his introduction of the rock star Dusty to Frederick for the ostensible purpose of engineering a sale of one of Frederick's artworks fools no one, especially not Lee, who realizes he really wants to see her. Conveying Frederick's extraordinary arrogance – "I don't sell my works by the yard!" (p. 78) – as well as Elliot's awkwardness, Allen once again evidences great compactness in his fusion of complex materials. And yet neither Elliot nor Frederick, as played by the classic Ingmar Bergman actor Max Von Sydow, can be casually dismissed as mere stock figures. Frederick, in spite of his faults, has sympathetic qualities. In confessing to Lee that she is his "only connection to the world" (p. 105), he presents an accurate, if brief, portrayal of the unrecognized man of genius whose powers of moral prescience recognize universal weakness but fail to achieve the same vision in the world immediately around him. He remains blind to the impossibility of his combined role as Lee's lover, teacher, and jailer. He also seems blind to his own surroundings. Allen gives the interior of his artist's loft a sense of bleak and boring blandness that easily can be imagined as a sort of prison for Lee. Even the wall of books seems foreboding rather than potentially stimulating, especially given Frederick's character. He insists on his right "to complete an education I started on you five years ago" (p. 103), realizing only too late that she dropped his course finally for another major with Elliot.

Even more than Frederick, Elliot achieves a depth and complexity of character that give him a significant place in the film. Deemed by Frederick to be "a glorified accountant" (p. 27) with an unwholesome lust for Lee, Elliot actually comes off as much more than Frederick's jealous and contemptuous characterization of him. He is, after all, the object of Hannah's desire, love, and hopes, and to give him credibility as such Allen needs to develop even the comic side of his character seriously. Thus, once we get past his awkwardness with Lee, we see him as a man of intelligence and sensitivity. He embodies the modern urbanite – most especially the upper-class New Yorker – of split personality divided between work and soul. He clearly loves the arts and literature and studies them for personal fulfillment rather than an ostentatious display of erudition as do characters in other Allen films. At the same time, Allen takes pains to demonstrate Elliot's authentic devotion to poetry and music, interests that he happily displays to manipulate Lee's feelings toward him. He knows e. e. cummings's "somewhere i have never travelled,gladly beyond":

your slightest look easily will
unclose me
though I have closed myself as
fingers,
you open always petal by petal
myself as Spring opens
(touching skillfully, mysteriously)
her first rose
(i do not know what it is about you
that closes and opens;
only something in me understands
the voice of your eyes is deeper than
all roses)...nobody, not even the rain, has such small hands

(pp. 63–4)

He also can instantly recognize Bach's F Minor Concerto (p. 80).

Caine makes Elliot's moral and emotional dilemma concerning his conflicting relationships with and feelings for Hannah and Lee quite human
and believable. In contrast to Frederick, who presumably sees and knows
the truth, Elliot's interior consciousness becomes a battleground of doubt
and guilt. Acting selfishly and compulsively, Elliot still remains capable of
moral sensitivity. At the same time, he also clearly lacks the moral courage
and fortitude to choose. At home in the bedroom with Hannah after sleeping
with Lee, his mixture of feelings about the afternoon's spent passion and
the evening's domestic comfort quickly accelerate to guilt and self-
recrimination: "She gives me a very deep feeling of being part of something.
She's a wonderful woman...and I betrayed her. She came into my empty
life and changed it...and I paid her back by banging her sister in a hotel
room" (p. 106). His thoughts assume a tone reminiscent of Hamlet: "God,
I'm despicable. What a cruel and shallow thing to do." At the same time,
trying to understand the human costs of his actions, he thinks almost like
a banker about weighing and comparing degrees of pain and hurt. With his
conscience pressing him ever harder about his "immoral" behavior and
feelings, he decides, "I'd rather hurt Lee a little, than destroy Hannah" (p.
107). Of course, he remains incapable for much of the film of resolving his
problem, until finally compelled to see Allen's inevitable repository of social
wisdom and moral insight, the psychotherapist: "I – I can't seem to take
action. I'm – I'm like, uh, Hamlet unable to kill his uncle....I want Lee,
but I can't harm Hannah. And in no other area am I a procrastinator" (p.
143). In this session with his therapist, Elliot then utters one of the film's

key lines: "For all my education, accomplishments, and so-called wisdom ...I can't fathom my own heart" (p. 144).

Elliot's turn to a therapist for help is fitting if unhelpful because his conflicting drives toward Hannah and Lee reflect tensions between the sisters involving classic Freudian ambivalences of love and authority. Positioning himself between Hannah's and Lee's latent roles as mother and daughter exacerbates the perverse intensity of his love for both women. Lee is the perennial student, what her mother calls the "ingenue" (p. 90). Indeed, the absence of her mother as a strong figure perhaps helps to account for such prolonged adolescence. In any case, her attitude to Elliot continues the pattern she established with Frederick: "I want you to take care of me... And I love when you do things to me" (p. 100). Characteristically, when she ultimately leaves Elliot because of his indecisiveness, it will be to go to a real teacher, her literature professor, Doug, at Columbia University. Ironically, this leaves Hannah in the position of fighting the battle for her husband and family, for whom she temporarily abandoned her career, with the very weapons of motherhood that have so alienated her from others who resent her dominance and strength. Indeed, her very position of authority within the family and her sense of responsibility toward others isolate her when it comes to her own needs. Thus, Holly tells her that she should "share" her problems with her sisters because she would "like to be bothered" (pp. 151–2), and Elliot cruelly tells her, "It's hard to be around someone who gives so much and – and needs so little in return!" When she responds in genuine confusion and pain, "But, look...I – I have enormous needs," he quickly snaps, "Well, I can't see them, and neither can Lee or Holly!" (p. 157).

Hannah's terrible sense of loss and confusion during these exchanges with Holly and Elliot, which occur during the second Thanksgiving celebration at her home, leaves her emotionally drained and psychologically naked in the midst of her own family. It takes place when her relationships with Elliot and her sisters seem to have reached their lowest point. However, the perdurability of her commitments also has had an effect on the situation, and her strengths of nurturing and love actually have gone deeper than the animosities that surround her. The power of these qualities of nurturance, endurance, and love are exhibited in an earlier dinner scene. This scene is exceptional for its ability to convey genuine emotion and pain without reverting to sentimentality, exaggerated feelings and behavior, or other artificial devices. Farrow is brilliant and absorbing in it. She demonstrates loss and abandonment without falling into hopeless pathos. The object of abuse, she does not fade into helpless victimization. Tortured by his conflicts and guilts, Elliot has been particularly detached and indifferent at dinner. When Hannah presses him, he resists. She says, "Are you angry with me?" "Do you feel, um... are you disenchanted with our marriage?" "Are you in love with someone else?" (p. 119). When she confesses that she would be "destroyed" if he answered yes to those questions, Elliot's conscience calls him to task: "For Chrissakes, stop torturing her. Tell her you want out and get it over with. You're in love with her sister. You didn't do it on purpose. Be honest. It's always the best way" (p. 120). However, when Hannah then turns to him both tenderly and lovingly to help rather than berate him, she has begun to win her battle, a battle that some viewers probably would prefer to see her abandon for independence from both the family and men. She says, "Look, can I help you? If you're suffering over something, will you share it with me?" Of course, Elliot cannot share it because to do so would destroy not only their marriage, but perhaps her relationships to her sister and family as well. Instead, he turns to her in love, although still not ready to commit himself totally to her: "Hannah, you know how much I love you. (*Kissing her on the forehead*) I ought to have my head examined. I don't deserve you" (p. 121). The scene ends with him kissing her again and holding her tightly. "(*She touches his hair*)" (p. 121).

Hannah's role in this scene is important, not just in terms of her relationship to Elliot, but also for its function in the film. It centralizes her power both contextually as a mother figure and structurally as the ultimate focus and source of desire. She becomes the defining force for the parallel narratives. She draws them all toward her, giving the film its special sense of direction and confirming Mickey's secondary role of comic support. Her power and authority are consistent with Allen's intention to make this a movie about women rather than himself. The focus on the female subject that dominates the structure and narrative of the film achieves special visual and emotional strength in what justifiably has become one of the most discussed and cited scenes in the movie. Significantly, the occasion for the scene involves Hannah, who has called the other sisters together for lunch. During the gathering, she remains the source of the action. The others are drawn toward her, even though she sometimes diplomatically disguises her motives. Thinking the lunch would be a good gathering to help Holly, she tells Lee, "I hope you can tell her it was your idea...'cause every time I try to be helpful, you know, sh – she gets so defensive" (p. 135). Trying to be independent of Hannah, even when you most need her, turns out to be a characteristic of both of her sisters.

The scene has become famous partly because of Allen's use of the camera that circles around the table as the women talk. The circular motion of the camera captures the conflicts, confusions, and concerns of the sisters. With this camera in motion, the form of the visualization for the scene embodies the tensions and anxieties that are circulating within and around the sisters. At the same time, the psychological thrust finds its direction toward Hannah. In a sense, she remains their sun as they circle around her, Holly by verbally assaulting Hannah for her questions about another career change – this one toward writing, which will turn out to be the right one – and Lee through her guilty feelings for betraying Hannah with Elliot. Holly's argument with Hannah follows the old pattern of Holly's dependence and defensiveness, while Lee's sympathy for Hannah constitutes her old mixture of young sisterly idealization and guilt over secret envy. Lee's silence through most of the discussion forms a shield for her secret and supports her role as the reticent youngest of the group who speaks up least.

However, what is most novel about the scene besides the camera technique is what is missing – men, no Elliot, no Frederick, no Mickey, no Doug, and no Dad. The women get together in a way that men in the film never can manage. In doing this, the women ultimately will be able to confront the dangers that threaten to overwhelm them. Therefore, along with psychic confusion, the circling camera also signals female and family circles of care, comfort, and community. As the camera continues to circle, Lee literally declares her dizziness and demands the end of the argument between Hannah and Holly so that they can eat. Without verbalizing the real sources of their tensions, they have agreed to come together.

In psychological terms, a direct link exists between this wish for sisterly community and at least two other developments: the growing relationship between Lee and her professor and Elliot's reconciliation with Hannah on the night of the Thanksgiving dinner. On that night, Hannah goes to bed feeling thoroughly alone because of her confrontations with Holly and Elliot. The room is dark after Elliot turns off the light. Hannah says off-screen, "It's so pitch-black tonight. I feel lost." Elliot responds by both turning the lamp on and turning to Hannah: "You're not lost. I love you so much" (p. 158). We will see that by the next Thanksgiving celebration, he finally has made peace with himself. However, the precipitating element in that reconciliation with Hannah has not been Elliot, who remains ambivalent and indecisive, but the women, Lee by finding a new lover-teacher and Hannah through the strength and endurance of her love.

The sisters' lunch, which helps to launch Holly on her new writing career, also sets the stage for another form of reconciliation through her accidental meeting with Mickey at a record store. Their fight during their date provides the basis for a new relationship that leads to their marriage and her eventual pregnancy, the ultimate signal for the end of his isolation. That news, given to him during the final Thanksgiving evening, caps off Mickey's analysis of his new domestic situation as he explains it to Holly: "I – I used to always have Thanksgiving with Hannah ... and I never thought (*Kissing*) that I could love anybody else. (*Kissing*) And here it is, years later and I'm married to you (*Kissing*) and completely in love with you. (*Kissing*)" This insight prompts him to echo Elliot's earlier words: "The heart is a very, very resilient little muscle. (*Kissing*) It really is" (p. 180). At the beginning of his new relationship with Holly, he had recounted to her how watching a Marx Bros. movie made him understand that life could be lived and enjoyed even without access to final meaning and truth, an experience that repeats Ike's apocalyptic vision of Tracy's face as the most important of many things that make life worth living. In truth, however, more has been accomplished. The film has been moving toward an acceptance of Hannah's position of love – or the heart. Both Mickey and Holly finally escape their isolation and depression through the power of love for renewal. Thus, the source of so much pain and uncertainty also becomes its own cure.

The conclusion of *Hannah and Her Sisters* led Maureen Dowd to ask in her *Sunday New York Times* piece, "Has Woody Allen turned some sort of emotional corner now, writing endings rosy with redemption and happily ever after?"[6] At least one of his lead actresses, Barbara Hershey, seemed to think so: "That kind of sweet ending really moved me," she told Dowd. Mia Farrow, however, answered the question with a better perspective and understanding of Allen's attitude and history as an artist: "He would hate to hear that."

These comments by Hershey and Farrow reiterate in a generous and receptive way the dilemma Allen faces with his critical and popular audiences. Allen's work since *Play It Again, Sam* steers between the extremes of two contrasting sets of alienated viewers who attack his work and credibility: those who want the old Woody of zany comedy to return and those who want a new Woody to make movies that reflect the current taste for skeptical cynicism. The ending of *Hannah and Her Sisters* probably would satisfy neither of these groups. Instead, the film as a whole, as well as its conclusion, reaffirms the unique vision and voice of his best work. Avoiding the sober, Bergmanesque brooding of some of his recent films, the conclusion of *Hannah and Her Sisters* still does not signal a concession to the demand for happy endings. The authenticity, artistic integrity, and compact structure of the film contradict such charges of compromise. On the other hand, a commitment to absolute darkness, which might satisfy other critics, would constitute a concession to simple explanations. For Allen, a view of life that sees only the darkness suggests a compromise with the challenge to see life whole. *Hannah and Her Sisters* indicates that Allen includes both light and dark. His darker moods certainly evidence his awareness of "the abyss," but his work also dramatizes our ability to love, laugh, and survive. For some in his audience, this balance places much of Allen's work on those lists his own screen characters sometimes make of experiences that contribute to the meaning and value of life.

Notes

1. Eric Lax, "Woody Allen–Not Only a Comic," *New York Times,* Sunday, February 24, 1985, Section 2, p. 24.

2. Walter Blair, "Mark Twain and the Mind's Ear," *The American Self: Myth, Ideology and Popular Culture,* ed. Sam B. Girgus (Albuquerque: University of New Mexico Press, 1981), p. 233.

3. Woody Allen, *Hannah and Her Sisters* (New York: Vintage, 1987), p. 5. All subsequent references to this film will be to this edition and will be included parenthetically in the text.

4. Graham McCann, *Woody Allen: New Yorker* (Cambridge: Polity, 1990), p. 235, says, "Allen's models for his narrative are Chekhov (for his musical texture and multiple points of view) and Tolstoy's *Anna Karenina* (for its parallel plot lines: first, an adulterous affair, second people's quest for meaning and happiness)."

5. Maureen Dowd, "The Five Women of *Hannah and Her Sisters,*" *New York Times,* Sunday, February 2, 1986, Section 2, pp. 1, 23.

6. Ibid., p. 33.

6
The Eyes of God

Many critics and writers did not overlook Woody Allen's use – or abuse – of vision as a metaphor for moral insight and blindness in *Crimes and Misdemeanors*. As Mary Erler, associate professor of English at Fordham University, wrote in the *Sunday New York Times*:

> In the movie's opening scene, a testimonial dinner, the ophthalmologist Judah Rosenthal tells us he has always remembered his father's warning that God's eyes see everything – and in fact that may be why he became an eye doctor. Our hearts sink, as we see that the movie intends to link the largest of moral questions – Is there a God? Is there a moral order? Is right action in the world rewarded and evil punished? – with the exhausted metaphor of vision as moral understanding. With an ophthalmologist as hero, will it be possible to escape a certain heavy-handedness in pursuit of these themes?[1]

Allen's oversimplification of such profound moral and philosophical questions certainly deserves some of Erler's criticism. Nevertheless, in spite of Allen's questionable development of this metaphor, the treatment of moral vision in *Crimes and Misdemeanors* requires further comment. Fortunately, Allen's directorial ingenuity and visual creativity in this film are not restricted to this cliché of vision and moral prescience and blindness. Allen goes beyond this metaphor to make another breakthrough movie, a film that includes humor but successfully emphasizes interior consciousness and moral ambiguity.

In the first place, the film explores an issue of key importance to Allen that has not been developed in comparable depth and detail in his previous work, namely Jewishness. As Rabbi Eugene B. Borowitz wrote, "A synagogue – better, a shul – a rabbi, a seder, a Jewish wedding, all receive respectful, even loving, treatment."² This use of Jewish materials in *Crimes and Misdemeanors* suggests a new quality of self-recognition on Allen's part, a moment of mature psychological insight into himself and his work. The roots for this "shock of recognition," however, can be found in some of his then-recent films.³ Allen's affectionate presentation of the nebbish agent in *Broadway Danny Rose* and his sentimentally sympathetic portrayal of a lower-middle-class Jewish family in *Radio Days* anticipate his serious presentation of Jewish identity and themes in *Crimes and Misdemeanors*.

Without compromising his critical detachment, Allen in *Crimes and Misdemeanors* seriously uses Jewish institutions and rituals as a means for discussing and debating the film's moral and philosophical concerns. This provides an enriching and reinforcing social and cultural context for the development of Allen's characters who are the kind of Jewish professionals, intellectuals, and artists that frequently appear in his films. Treating them seriously as Jewish characters and paying so much attention to their identity as Jews give them a sense of place and situation that similar figures in other Allen films often lack. Here we get repeated flashbacks to Judah Rosenthal's Jewish upbringing with a scholarly father named Sol who lectures the future ophthalmologist about righteousness and the omniscience of God. A flashback to a Passover seder becomes a provocative debate over religion, faith, justice, and political power. Here also, Allen dons a yarmulke as a sign of religious observance and participation during a Jewish wedding ceremony that structures the ending of the film. To his artistic and intellectual credit, Allen does not merely parade these scenes before us in the patronizing way that other directors often use Jewish themes to appeal to what they think Jewish and non-Jewish audiences want or expect to see. Moral irony, ambiguity, and uncertainty pervade these scenes, thereby adding a critical perspective and skeptical dimension to the security and certainty that such religious rituals and situations are designed to convey. The film's attempt to examine and question the terms of its own discourse constitutes perhaps its strongest sign of respect for and serious treatment of Jewish subjects and experiences.

However, anyone familiar with Allen's work over the years can readily recall a countermovement in his films that has not always indicated such comfort with and respect toward Jewish themes. The portrayal of a rabbi in *Everything You Always Wanted to Know About Sex* offended or at least bothered many Jewish fans. Using a game show parody as his format, Allen puts a rabbi in the humiliating situation of answering "What's My Perversion?" As Douglas Brode writes, "The sequence is burdened by the problem of image-following-the-verbal-gag, as when we hear the announcer say that the rabbi's secret fantasy is to be bound and whipped by a shiksa goddess while his wife is forced to eat pork." Brode goes on to describe this as an "undeniably funny" line "if in a cruel and, for a Jew, self-despising kind of way."[4] In *Annie Hall,* a mixture of paranoia and embarrassment colors the treatment of Jews and Jewish identity. In *Hannah and Her Sisters,* Mickey confesses to his parents that part of his reason for considering conversion to Catholicism can be explained "because I got off to a wrong foot with my own thing, you know."[5] More interesting and telling perhaps, is a nervous pause, a pregnant hesitation of self-consciousness in Mickey when he tells a Hare Krishna leader, "Well, I was born Jewish, you know, but, uh, but last winter I tried to become a Catholic and . . . it didn't work for me."[6]

At the very least, such literary and visual representations of Jewish subjects suggest ambivalence and conflict at the heart of the Jewish theme in Allen's movies. The intensity of this ambivalence ironically becomes clearer in a self-deceiving statement in which Allen denies the importance to him and his work of being Jewish. In an interview for an article about Allen, which appeared in the *New York Times Magazine* in 1979, Natalie Gittelson reports that, according to Allen, "the fact of being Jewish never consciously enters his work" and Jewish identity occupies only the "surfaces" of his films. He says:

> It's not on my mind: it's no part of my artistic consciousness. There are certain cultural differences between Jews and non-Jews, I guess, but I think they're largely superficial. Of course, any character I play would be Jewish, just because I'm Jewish. I'm also metropolitan oriented. I wouldn't play a farmer or an Irish seaman. So I write about metropolitan characters who happen to be Jewish.[7]

Such dismissal and trivialization of the influence of Jewishness upon his work seem remarkable. Universally identified by critics and audiences as a Jewish figure since the beginning of his career, Allen has consciously manipulated this aspect of his public persona and his creative characterizations in almost all of his work ranging from his best stand-up comedy, to his *New Yorker* magazine pieces and, of course, his films. It seems to me, therefore, that in this 1979 article, Allen evidences a considerable degree of denial and blindness about this aspect of his life and work. His treatment of Jewish materials in much of his work, as already noted, frequently tends to confirm this tendency toward emotional ambivalence, disguise, and denial. Accordingly, *Crimes and Misdemeanors* seems to signify a milestone of both a personal and creative sort for Allen in opening up and identifying sources of creativity and being, as well as insecurity and unhappiness.

If Allen's treatment of Jewish themes suggests a certain maturity in *Crimes and Misdemeanors,* he also aspires to fulfill an aesthetic standard in this film that has been his goal as a director and writer for years. This creative objective for Allen can be understood in terms of his analysis of the achievement of Ingmar Bergman, the director Allen most passionately admires and would most like to emulate. As Gittelson reports, "The moviemaker Allen ranks highest is Ingmar Bergman. Bergman's gloom is, spiritually, Allen's gloom." She goes on to quote Allen:

I have a personal taste for the mood he sets. That's my kind of good evening. He makes innovative, cinematic, magnificent, strong, high dramas. In this or that film, he may have missed out. But 12 or 15 masterpieces, in varying degrees, out of 40 pictures? That's astounding![8]

Clearly, Bergman's influence upon Allen can be seen in *Interiors* as well as in more recent films such as *Another Woman* and *September.* For Allen, Bergman succeeds in making great movies in the genre and form that Allen most respects, tragedy. He told Gittelson, "Tragedy is a form to which I would ultimately like to aspire. I tend to prefer it to comedy. Comedy is easier for me. There's not the same level of pain in its creation, or the confrontation with issues or with oneself, or the working through of ideas."[9]

Many critics have derided and many fans have expressed disappointment in Allen's turn to Bergman's tragic vision of life and cinema. In essence, they see this interest as a sign of intellectual and creative pretension, a kind of aesthetic midlife crisis suggestive of a deeper insecurity that causes him to aspire for success as a major artist in the presumably more serious and challenging genre of tragedy. For such critics, Allen's apparent need for artistic and creative recognition in his alleged area of weakness, drama and tragedy, sadly takes time and energy from his true genius and gift, comedy. As Pauline Kael in the *New Yorker* says of Allen's films: "Not so long ago, Woody Allen movies were awaited with joy; then he began to make tasteful versions of Ingmar Bergman pictures. He has a new one, *Another Woman,* and – Well, I didn't much care for *Wild Strawberries* the first time."[10] Similarly, Tom Shales – in an article significantly subtitled "Is America's nebbish auteur taking himself too seriously? Funny you should ask" – writes, "His audience can't vote, no, on what Woody Allen will do or who Woody

Allen will be. But maybe he could give them a little credence, a little attention or, say, just a little sympathy."[11]

Fortunately, Allen's self-imposed pressure, as noted earlier, to "stretch" himself artistically apparently offsets the oppressive weight of the ridicule and derision from such negative writers and reviewers. Allen's interest in Bergman, which so easily arouses sarcastic condescension, remains inseparable in his mind from his development as a director and artist. He obviously sees himself as using Bergman to develop the materials and methods of directing in ways that not only challenge his artistic growth, but also enable him to construct and reconstruct a visual engagement with the world and experience. Thus, Allen's recent review of *The Magic Lantern*, Bergman's autobiography, delineates by implication his own artistic and theoretical aspirations. In writing about Bergman, Allen in effect writes his own story and theory of film as well. In this review, Allen also elaborates upon his ideas of tragedy, at least as they relate to Bergman's work.

In the review, Allen articulates a kind of artistic double vision for himself and Bergman involving a theoretical distinction between the technique and art of directing, on the one hand, and the substantive content and moral imagination of a particular work, on the other. As we have seen, Allen's most successful films, such as *Manhattan, Annie Hall,* and *Hannah and Her Sisters,* embody the integration of technique and artistry with moral and thematic development. The distinction between style and substance, however, remains a useful one for him. In his review of Bergman's autobiography, Allen explains the need for "a digression here about style." He argues that, for a long time, it seemed natural that "the predominant arena for conflict" for film was "the external, physical world" because the camera could capture that domain so readily and with so much more seeming accuracy than other media. Films during this stage, he maintains, developed such "staples" as "slapstick and westerns, war films and chases and gangster movies and musicals."[12]

However, as suggested by Allen's own work in *Zelig,* such confidence in the camera's ability to capture the essence of external reality would not go unquestioned or unchallenged. Moreover, this emphasis upon external reality and conflict eventually changed with a new interest in using film and the camera to explore the psyche and the realm of interior emotion and conflict. Allen writes:

> As the Freudian revolution sank in, however, the most fascinating arena of conflict shifted to the interior, and films were faced with a

problem. The psyche is not visible. If the most interesting fights are being waged in the heart and mind, what to do?"[13]

Allen, obviously, is well aware that, throughout history, artists and writers have concentrated precisely on this arena of internal, hidden conflict. It also should not go unnoticed that he attributes the major shift in modern thought and perception to Freud, the one thinker whose presence and dominance can be felt throughout his work. His major point here, however, is that in the relatively new art of cinema, Bergman, according to Allen, created a new way of filmmaking to explore this world of inner consciousness, feeling, and turmoil. He writes, "Bergman evolved a style to deal with the human interior, and he alone among directors has explored the soul's battlefield to the fullest." For Allen, Bergman's great innovation in dramatizing interior consciousness involves his use of the close-up:

> One saw great performers in extreme close-ups that lingered beyond where the textbooks say is good movie form. Faces were everything for him. Close-ups. More close-ups. Extreme close-ups. He created dreams and fantasies and so deftly mingled them with reality that gradually a sense of the human interior emerged. He used huge silences with tremendous effectiveness.[14]

Arguing that "the terrain of Bergman films is different from his contemporaries," Allen maintains, "He has found a way to show the soul's landscape." Allen also believes that "by rejecting cinema's standard demand for conventional action, he has allowed wars to rage inside characters that are as acutely visual as the movement of armies."[15]

Allen describes Bergman as a sort of Columbus of directors who was the first to explore and open to large and appreciative audiences an unknown inner terrain of emotion and conflict. In his enthusiasm for Bergman, Allen in this review obviously overlooks an impressive list of directors who preceded Bergman in the use of the close-up, beginning probably with D. W. Griffith. Nevertheless, Allen's understanding of the Swedish director's enormous contribution to cinema helps to explain the direction of Allen's work for more than a decade. Clearly, many of his own cinematic innovations, from *Play It Again, Sam* to *Annie Hall* and *Manhattan,* represent his desire to expose and dramatize the inner domain of psychic conflict and alienation in the manner of Bergman. The revolution of subjectivity and sexuality in *Play It Again, Sam,* the representation of psychic division through the use of such devices as the split screen in *Annie Hall,* the presentation and dramatization of displacement and decenteredness on the Scope-screen in

Manhattan, and the circling camera in *Hannah and Her Sisters* all involve attempts to realize interior tensions and latent conflicts on the screen. Certainly the influence on Allen of other important directors besides Bergman can be seen in these films. Fellini's interest in fantasy and social criticism, De Sica's documentary vision, and Welles's camera technique are present in Allen's work. Nevertheless, it remains significant that, in Allen's view, Bergman stands as the most important to him, at least as a source for the depiction of internal conflict and interior consciousness.

Moreover, Allen's great appreciation for Bergman's method of dramatizing interior consciousness helps to explain his vulnerability to the cliché of the visual metaphor for moral understanding and insight in *Crimes and Misdemeanors.* For him, the metaphor of vision into the unknown concerns not only the examination of the moral dimension of human experience. It also becomes a metaphor for the artistic process behind his entire filmmaking project. The "eyes of God," a phrase from *Crimes and Misdemeanors,* describes precisely how he wants the camera and his filmmaking to look within and to bring out that world for art.

Also, the visual metaphor for moral issues and the visual metaphor for the acts of directing and filmmaking merge in Allen's interest in moving from comedy to tragedy. As we have seen, in many of his films humor provides a valuable dramatic mechanism to avoid direct and immediate confrontation with the very issues, fears, and conflicts that such humor implies and presents. This technique of humor operates throughout *Annie Hall* in which the humor structures indirection as a means for expressing the latent and unknown. Such humor, it has been argued, often shapes Allen's treatment of the Jewish materials and subjects already discussed. This even occurs in *Manhattan* when Ike expresses his fears to his best friend Yale over how quitting his job will drastically alter his way of life. He says:

> I mean, you know, oh . . . plus I'll probably have to give my parents less money. You know, this is gonna kill my father. He's gonna – he's not gonna be able to get as good a seat in the synagogue, you know. . . . This year he's gonna be in the back, away from God, far from the action.[16]

Here the joke relieves the appropriate tension but dramatizes the fear Ike feels, while also suggesting deeper sources for his insecurity involving his vulnerability and manhood as a provider and his marginalization as a Jew. A clear example of humorous indirection in its deflection of latent fears and concerns, the joke also typifies the humor of Allen's films since *Play It*

Again, Sam. For Allen, humor in these films is dramatic, situational, and contextual. It operates as part of a broader strategy to develop character and drama within a context of complex questions and relationships. Allen's turn to Bergman, therefore, is consistent with his attempt to integrate humor and sadness in his work, partly through a more direct confrontation with the dark complexity of the difficult issues raised in his films. Like Ike's father, at least part of Allen now prefers to find a place where God will not have to search him out.

The question reasserts itself at this point as to whether Allen overcomes his own cliché of the visual metaphor in *Crimes and Misdemeanors* through his creative use of the camera to explore and express the interior domain that he regards as the greatest challenge to a modern director. In this film, how successfully does he follow Bergman in finding "a way to show the soul's landscape"?

We can begin answering these questions by noting that Allen devises a familiar narrative structure for *Crimes and Misdemeanors* that provides a useful vehicle for the visual exploration of internal psychological situations. As in *Manhattan* and *Hannah and Her Sisters,* Allen uses parallel stories to construct his larger narrative; the narratives ultimately merge through the relationships the characters have with each other and through the dramatic development of the film's interconnected themes. To typical Allen stories of love and rejection, he now adds new elements of evil and the sinister. One narrative concerns the turmoil in the internal and external lives of Judah, the successful ophthalmologist, played flawlessly by Martin Landau. Judah must deal with the threats of his mistress Dolores, played by Anjelica Huston, to ruin him if he refuses to abandon his wife, portrayed by Claire Bloom, who appears only briefly. The second narrative line essentially concerns Allen's character, Cliff Stern, an idealistic, but unsuccessful nebbish filmmaker, who pursues the Mia Farrow character, Halley Reed, but loses her to a successful and famous figure that Stern detests named Lester, played by Alan Alda in the film's second great performance. As in *Hannah and Her Sisters,* Allen's story provides a comic countermovement to the dark and sinister story of Judah. The music for the first story tends toward Franz Schubert, while the comic tone of Allen's competition with Alda over Farrow finds support in lively jazz. Like Mickey in *Hannah,* Cliff's relationship to these people is primarily that of an outsider through a fragile marriage. Cliff's marriage to Lester's sister, Wendy, who is played by Joanna Gleason, teeters on a precipice of divorce, sustained for the moment only by their mutual emotional inertia. Wendy's other brother, Ben, played by Sam Waterston, is the prophetic and morally sensitive rabbi whose advancing blindness compels him to go for help and treatment to Judah, a social and family friend.

As in Allen films that go back at least to *Play It Again, Sam* and *Annie Hall*, in *Crimes and Misdemeanors* narrative often progresses in unconventional ways. Instead of advancing consistently according to traditional narrative continuity, the film frequently cuts from various scenes and enters into new ones to construct psychological, thematic, and moral connections. The film cuts from Dolores's compelling rage and hysteria in one scene to another of rather crass symbolism with the rabbi, Ben, as he follows a pin dot light in the pitch-black darkness of Judah's office during an eye examination. Of course, the examination of the rabbi's eyes quickly evolves into a study of the dark condition of the doctor's soul as he confesses his anxiety and guilt over his affair with Dolores. In both of these scenes, we see emotional chaos and a blind search for justice. Elsewhere in the film, we cut from a scene between Halley and Cliff in which she smartly puts down his modest advance and compliment to a scene with his sister, Barbara, who describes a humiliating act performed against her by a man she met through a personals column. These scenes deal with rejection and the quest for love. While Barbara's description of her depressing loneliness underscores Cliff's own barren existence, it also renders emotional and psychological credibility to Dolores's desperate actions, which are motivated by her consuming fear of the impending emptiness of her life without Judah. Barbara explains to Cliff, "You don't know what it's like to be by yourself all the time," without realizing that, in a sense, Cliff is always by himself. Similarly, the narrative also often develops through the juxtaposition of scenes that contrast radically with each other in terms of mood, moral message, or personal relationships. For example, the movie cuts from Judah's telephone call, during which he tells his brother, Jack, played by Jerry Orbach, to proceed with their plans to murder Dolores, to a funny scene with Alda pompously pontificating about experience and life as he walks down a New York street to the accompaniment of "Sweet Georgia Brown."

Freed from the rigid bonds of traditional plot development, Allen's method of narrative organization allows him to explore the potential in particular scenes for the visual dramatization of interior realms that he espouses in his review of Bergman. To meet this challenge for the visual psychological development of character, Allen employs what can be called a form of interior camera from the beginning of *Crimes and Misdemeanors*. His technique involves a systematic use and interconnection of close-ups and flashbacks to explore and chart this interior geography. This artistic "style," to use Allen's word, operates with powerful authority and effect, becoming a visual motif that runs throughout the film. Indeed, the sustained sophistication, subtlety, and precision of Allen's method of interweaving close-ups and flashbacks suggest impressive visual and stylistic maturity on his part. The great success of this method to some extent replaces Allen's technical and visual innovations such as the Scope-screen and split screen in previous films. In *Crimes and Misdemeanors,* the emphasis stays on the search for interior meaning and reality.

Crimes and Misdemeanors opens with a scene that briefly exhibits the social landscape of a dinner in honor of Judah, but quickly moves to a close-up and flashback that gets us directly into Judah's mind. The public celebration of Judah's philanthropy, service to his community, brilliance, charm, and savoir-faire conflict radically with the internal drama of adultery, fear, and guilt that plays in his mind as he recalls that just before the evening's dinner, he found a letter from his mistress to his wife detailing the adulterous affair and demanding action to resolve the situation. In Judah's flashback, Allen's tight camera concentrates on ever more specific details that dramatize the internal tension. While Dolores's voice-over renders the letter's contents, a frontal shot shows Judah's hands holding the letter; his white shirt, tie, and belt provide the background. Without Judah's head in the shot, the camera seems to put our eyes on the letter, in a sense, therefore, putting us both into the letter and into the eyes that are reading it. "The situation has got to be confronted in some fashion," the letter says. When we return to the dinner and Judah's urbane speech, a momentary flashback illustrates his words about his religious upbringing so that we see the synagogue of his youth where his father told him, "The eyes of God are on us always." Throughout the film, Allen uses flashbacks in this way for instant illustrations as well as for extended interior journeys. They provide visual confirmation of one of the film's themes of the presence of the past in our daily lives.

At the same time, Allen does not rely solely upon this technique of flashbacks and close-ups to convey the psychological state and situation of his characters. In the scene that follows the testimonial dinner, Allen will again put us in Judah's place after we track Dolores as she walks down a New York City street toward her apartment. Then an interior shot in her apartment focuses on the apartment door, forcing us to wait for her arrival. It also should be noted that the shots in this apartment immediately provide powerful visualizations of an internal state of tension, compression, distortion, and blindness. Allen's use of interior space here compares to similar scenes in *Manhattan* and other films. An ugly metal bookcase makes the narrow foyer by the door especially confining. The organization of the apartment and its furnishings interrupt and distort vision and perception so that all the shots and scenes in this setting become dramatic visualizations of deception and partial truth. In a later scene in this apartment, a suspended microwave seems to decapitate Dolores so we hear her voice and see her body but not her face.

However, in the scene under discussion, the disturbing sense of fragmentation and division that the apartment conveys achieves its strongest punch as Dolores enters and we hear Judah's voice from off-screen. Both the viewer and Dolores are startled by the sound. The hidden Judah, whose possession of his own key to the apartment intimates the nature of his relationship with Dolores, enters the screen from the right. The use of camera and sound creates a feeling of sensory separation that reinforces the psychological division of the scene, while the interior shot puts us in the position of once again seeing what Judah sees but not quite being Judah. The interior shot puts us inside their relationship and his mind, while at the same time de-centering the characters and the viewer. Also in this apartment scene, when Judah and Dolores speak together, the camera frames the upper parts of their bodies, first, in a kind of window divider between the kitchen and living room that inevitably also interrupts and distorts our vision of them in other shots and, second, in shots before the spikelike and sterile vertical blinds of a long window. Both frames are confining and discomforting and evoke a feeling of pressure and threat that summarizes the emotional turmoil of the relationship. Thus, Dolores's apartment visually and spatially conveys the sense and feeling of what Judah's brother Jack in a different context calls a "deep, dark secret." The apartment seems as twisted and distorted as the truth and the human relationships in the film. It also should be noted that the apartment provides a marvelous contrast with the openness and brightness of the interior and exterior spaces and setting of Judah's home. Typically, in a flashback of Dolores's recollection of her happiness with Judah on a beach, when they hug, Judah immediately expresses his fear of public exposure in such an open and visible space.

The film's most powerful and moving moments occur when Allen contextualizes his method of flashbacks and close-ups in physical settings and dramatic situations that compound psychological and moral complexity and intensify emotional and moral tensions. In such moments, Allen does more than merely mix all these elements together into a kind of cinematic alchemy. Instead, he contrives an original artistic vision. Thus, Dolores's hysterical phone call to Judah from a roadside bar near his home sets up a scene of originality and power. Her call had interrupted a family celebration of his birthday by forcing him to leave to console her in a parked car during a terrible evening rainstorm.

Following this surreptitious and disturbing meeting, we find Judah alone in the middle of the night. In this scene, Allen dramatizes the internal battle within Judah so that the divided selves that comprise Judah's character debate each other. With flashes of lightning ominously illuminating the evening darkness of his home, Judah enters to the voice-over of Ben, in a kind of auditory flashback, repeating the moral advice he offered during the eye examination: "You have to confess the wrong and hope for understanding," the voice says. It repeats Ben's argument that only a belief in a moral structure to the universe makes life worthwhile. While we hear Ben's voice, the camera focuses on Judah's feet, creating a disconcerting effect of a truncated figure as Judah finally stops his restless pacing to sit on his couch. Ben's voice reiterates his faith in Judah's ultimate conviction in a moral basis to life and experience. He knows that a "spark of that notion is inside you somewhere too." As Judah lights a cigarette and stares from the couch into the dying embers in the fireplace, the voice asks if Judah could really go through with the murder. Then in a stroke of dramatic ingenuity, the dark figure of Ben enters from behind Judah and occupies a place in the corner of the room that leaves him visually in the scene over Judah's shoulder, the physical embodiment of the voice of conscience, a scene evocative of William Holman Hunt's famous pre-Raphaelite painting entitled *The Awakening Conscience* in which the conscience in the shape of a shadow inspires a girl to rise from the lap of her would-be seducer.

The figure of Ben appears as a visual representation of Judah's internalization of a conventional moral and religious conscience. Ben's voice and body personify typical moral authority and wisdom. However, they soon will function primarily to develop Judah's own inner discourse. In other words, when we first hear Ben's voice and then see him, he merely represents Judah's recapitulation and reconsideration of the various aspects of the moral and emotional crisis in his life. At this point, Ben embodies a traditional moralistic perspective that Judah internalizes, but ultimately will reject in favor of his own evil and ambition.

As this scene proceeds, therefore, we go more deeply into Judah's consciousness so that his own voice and true moral character emerge. When Judah debates Ben concerning his doubts, he literally puts words in the rabbi's mouth. The figure of Ben articulates Judah's consciousness, and the process of interior exploration to which Allen is so committed achieves a new depth and intensity. In a sense, we get Ben's voice without quotation marks since it reverberates in Judah's mind, an achievement comparable in terms of moral drama to the famous absence of quotation marks in *Huckleberry Finn* when Huck decides to disobey his official "deformed conscience" and to follow his "sound heart" and go to hell rather than allow the return of Jim to slavery.[17] This development of Judah's voice through Ben entails a major advance for Allen and a significant sign of his artistic maturity. Moreover, the comparison to Twain seems especially interesting because of the contrasting outcomes of the situations in the novel and the film. In the novel, of course, Huck's "sound heart" appears to win. In the film, the scene ends with Judah's decision to initiate the plan for Dolores's murder, thereby confirming the film's darker suggestions and fears of an evil world without moral certainty and true justice – a world without the promise of punishment, as implied in Dostoyevsky's novel, but with only varying degrees of crime and corruption. Judah tells Ben, who now has moved from the shadows and the corner to sit with him on the couch in order to engage in a serious discussion, "God is a luxury I can't afford." No longer a mere shadow or recollection of a previous conversation, but a living part of Judah's own mind and an embodiment of Judah's debate with himself, Ben suggests that Judah has come to sound like his brother Jack by talking with Jack's cynicism. Judah responds, "Jack lives in the real world. You live in the kingdom of heaven." In his despair, Judah tries to imagine what other advice Ben could possibly offer, but he concludes with his own voice and a sense of justice that defers to a more powerful hunger for survival as the camera focuses on the telephone, the visual sign of Judah's internal decision and forthcoming actions.

Through much of the film, perfectly timed flashbacks and close-ups convey the inner turmoil and guilt Judah initially feels over his terrible decision. These scenes tend to recall moments he shared with Dolores, including some that suggest real affection and excitement between them. However, in terms of setting and dramatic situation, one flashback compares in complexity and originality to the imaginary scene just described between Judah and Ben. This scene also compares to one in *Annie Hall* when Alvy Singer and his friends return to Alvy's boyhood home and together observe Alvy's family and past. In *Crimes and Misdemeanors,* Judah returns alone. To get there, he drives through a tunnel at the end of which he momentarily imagines the ark for the torah in his father's synagogue, a way of envisioning his future through past structures of guilt, conscience, and fear. When he arrives at the house, he explains his interest in revisiting his former home to the current occupant and tells the woman that he and his brother "were very close in those days," a comment that suggests a latent wish to separate himself in the present from his brother as though the recent murder does not form a bond between them. Ironically, Jack's behavior and acerbic comments in other scenes not only contradict Judah's words here regarding the past, but suggest that the murder in fact has brought Jack closer to his brother who, as Jack said earlier, always hated to get his "hands dirty." The murder indicates that the brothers are close in ways that Judah has preferred to deny or repress.

As Judah walks through the old house, he looks through a door into the past and an imaginary Passover seder at which different family members talk and debate vigorously about politics, religion, and morality. This seder to observe and celebrate the exodus of the Hebrews from Egypt includes impassioned debate over religious, Marxist, and humanistic perspectives of history and justice. When they argue over the issue of immoral acts and punishment, Judah interrupts. The family turns to him and Judah says, "If a man commits a crime, if he . . . if he kills . . . ," and his father Sol responds, "Then one way or another he will be punished." Sol refers to both the Old Testament and Shakespeare to proclaim that "murder will out," and Judah exclaims, "Who said anything about murder?" Again Sol answers with simple truth: "You did!" The family turns from Judah, who becomes a stranger to his own people and to himself, a modern-day biblical wanderer with his heavy burden of guilt and fear. Like a figure out of Poe, Judah indicts and convicts himself. The guilt, of course, resides in him, not just in Sol's moral pronouncements.

The seder scene provides another external dramatization of an internal psychic debate over conscience. The careful attention to the details of the seder supper gives a special edge to Judah's moral pain and anxiety at this moment. In this scene, emotion becomes tangible and palpable by connecting Judah's inner life to a concrete event filled with family history and cultural significance. Moreover, the scene beautifully enacts the ineluctable dilemma and tension involving the nature of the past that, by definition, remains remote and inaccessible, but nevertheless exists as an inseparable part of our internal lives and personal histories. Judah's search for unity and peace in his past only confirms his psychic and social separation. From a liminal position on the fringe of the room, he peers as an alien upon his family. He sees that he has everything and nothing. Since the days of his youth, he has achieved success, a measure of fame, the admiration of family and friends, but he also has no central identity and no place where he can openly be himself. And he decides that he can learn to exist as an absolute fraud as long as he can pretend to be everything that he is not.

In the film's earlier scene when Judah and Ben engage in an imaginary discourse, the rabbi as the embodiment of Judah's conscience asks Judah "could you sleep" with the knowledge of engineering the murder of another human: "Is that who you really are?" *Crimes and Misdemeanors* purports to engage this question of identity and morality for Judah and also for the other major characters such as Lester and Cliff. Judah overcomes his tortured conscience, manages to sleep, and by the end of the film is even amazed at how easy it is to achieve peace of mind, how much he really is like his brother.

Similarly, the film contrives a hilarious, if incomplete portrait of Lester in the form of Cliff's documentary about him. Viewing the film Cliff has made of him, Lester shrieks, "The idea was to show the real me!" Of course, "the real me" – or at least much of it – appears in the documentary: a womanizer who exploits female employees; an ill-tempered bully who fires a writer with cancer because he is no longer funny; a narcissist who dominates and humiliates all those around him. In this documentary, Cliff the failed filmmaker proffers a marvelous lesson in the power of art to achieve a stronger sense of truth than a strict adherence to so-called reality. By making visual comparisons of Lester to Mussolini and a talking mule, Cliff demonstrates the kind of visual inventiveness that Allen himself advocates and exemplifies as a director. As in his development of Judah, Allen also manages to place Lester in an important social and cultural context through Lester's screeching denial of Cliff's assertion in the documentary that Lester's use of media undermines democratic institutions and mature artistic sensibilities. This idea especially enrages Lester who presents himself to the public as a beneficent liberal consciousness. Quoting from Cliff's script, Lester shrieks, "I don't promote . . . values that deaden the sensibilities of a great democracy." In his rage, Lester almost physically removes Cliff from the scene as well as the documentary. The film also suggests mixed motivations behind Halley's choice of Lester over Cliff when she admits, earlier in the film, to being more "ambitious" about her career than Cliff realizes.

At the same time, *Crimes and Misdemeanors* conveys a dark side to Cliff's character that makes him more than a simple victim of heartless and callous figures who lack his sensitivity. Cliff assumes a moral superiority and enhanced artistic sensibility that he really does not prove or earn. He has a misplaced pride in failure, self-servingly imagining a degree of heroism in his recalcitrance to popular values and success. In fact, his compulsive passion for fleeing to daily afternoon movies masks his real resistance to competition and achievement and feeds into another compulsive need, for the attention and adulation of his young niece, Jennifer. By spending so much time with the young girl, Cliff persuades himself that he merely wants to fulfill his self-generated deathbed promise to her father to assume responsibility for her education. Actually, she serves as a convenient rationalization for his own self-indulgence. In his need for this girl's time and in his attraction to Halley – both of whom distract him from his creative and professional work and failing marriage – Cliff approximates the narcissism of the film's two putative villains, Judah and Lester. Cliff also shares a kind of blindness with Ben in which illusions substitute for truth. Like Isaac in *Manhattan*, Cliff loses the girl to a seemingly morally inferior character, while also failing to appreciate his own moral shortcomings.

Moreover, the film perceives and presents a degree of moral complexity and ambiguity in Judah and even in Lester. Thus, when Judah returns in his imagination to the family seder he encounters a significant diversity of views. However, the moral and philosophical positions that are voiced by those seated around the seder table tend to cancel each other out. The tough-minded realism of radical Marxism and the inspiring idealism of religious faith and humanism are offered as absolute and totalistic perspectives that, for Judah, seem tendentious and partial, thereby confirming his skepticism and sense of loss. He feels abandoned in a moral wilderness. Intellectual systems that make assertions of moral certainty no longer adequately describe or fit Judah's experience. As Halley says after the suicide of the moral philosopher who has been the subject of one of Cliff's moribund documentaries, all systems of belief "no matter how elaborate" ultimately seem "incomplete" when measured against the vicissitudes and uncertainties of lived experience. He cannot have blind faith either in God like his father or in the power of class warfare and historical determinism like his aunt. Thus, the film confronts the moral frontier of values and fears that provides an important context, although not a justification, for Judah's deceitful and atrocious actions.

Similarly, Lester possesses qualities that complicate the portrait of him presented in Cliff's documentary. There is a side to Lester that Cliff denies. Elements of generosity, creativity, and expansiveness in Lester's character perhaps make him at least as worthy of love and admiration as is Cliff. Speaking to Cliff, Halley says of Lester, "He's not what you think. He's... he's wonderful. He's warm and caring and romantic." She correctly bristles over Cliff's instinctive self-serving and self-justifying response that "He's a success. That's what he is. He's rich and he's a success." She fires back, "Oh... give me a little credit, will you?" When he in turn responds, "Well, I always did give you a little credit until today," Cliff's words ironically reveal the hidden strain of judgmental superiority in his attitude.

A strain of vintage Allen humor ripples steadily through *Crimes and Misdemeanors*. Gag lines and perfectly timed humor punctuate the dark themes and dramatic characterizations in the film. At the beginning of the film, Cliff is prepared to attack a cripple for a taxi. At the end of the film when he attends the wedding of Judah's daughter, he announces that everything on him is rented. And when he encounters Halley at the wedding with her new husband, Lester, he confesses, on her return of his love letter, that it's probably just as well to get it back since he plagiarized most of it from James Joyce, which explains the letter's many irrelevant references to Dublin. This humorous strain, in combination with Alda's triumphant portrayal of Lester, makes *Crimes and Misdemeanors* a truly funny film.

Although thoroughly successful and effective, this restrained use of humor never will satisfy those fans and critics who continue to yearn for the old Woody of endless sight gags and zany events and jokes. Allen, however, should feel considerable satisfaction with *Crimes and Misdemeanors*. In spite of the film's flaws, including perhaps the most egregious abuse of the metaphor of vision and moral blindness in the awful symbolism of the dimming headlights of Judah's car, he should regard the film as an artistic success. Perhaps his most complete artistic work, it fully integrates and balances humor and drama to convey his understanding of contemporary experience.

Crimes and Misdemeanors offers some self-reflexive consideration to the moral meaning of the film and the nature of film itself. Typically for Allen, the film includes a discussion of the art form in general and this film in particular. The discussion comes at the very end of the film during the wedding of Judah's daughter. Off by himself to contemplate his loss of Halley and the injustice of Lester's triumph, Cliff finally meets Judah, who also has wandered off in search of a moment of privacy. Thinking about his disappointment, Cliff confesses to Judah that he was plotting a "perfect murder," and Judah assumes that Cliff was considering a movie plot. Judah then offers his version of a perfect murder by reiterating the story we have just witnessed of *Crimes and Misdemeanors*. What follows amounts to a metacommentary on the film as they interpret the moral significance of the story and discuss both the nature of tragedy and the capacity of films to convey such a narrative. Significantly, Cliff misses the point, remaining true to his character in the film, while Judah evidences a prescience beyond Cliff's limited abilities. Cliff wants an ending to the story that fits his mistaken conception of tragedy in which the villain confesses and accepts existential responsibility for his actions, a view that, by the way, seems to contradict and oversimplify Allen's own discussion and understanding of tragedy in his review of Ingmar Bergman's autobiography. The idea of a villain who benefits from his evil and accommodates himself to his own duplicity, deception, and dishonesty makes Cliff uneasy. He prefers a neat ending, which he inaccurately dubs tragedy. However, the more insightful, but evil Judah smiles at his naïveté. What Cliff sees as tragedy, Judah describes as a happy ending. To Judah, Cliff sees life in terms of fiction and make-believe. He correctly surmises that "you see too many movies." He says, "I mean if you want a happy ending, you ... you should go see a Hollywood movie," the last thing someone with Cliff's intellectual ambitions and artistic pretensions wants to hear.

In sharp contrast to the film Cliff would like to see, Allen creates a film about contemporary ambiguity and uncertainty. There is no resolution, no ultimate reconstitution of moral meaning and structure. This vision of moral ambiguity and uncertainty is one that Allen has been advancing and developing in all of his major, mature films. And *Crimes and Misdemeanors* probably is his strongest and most coherent rendering of that vision and understanding of experience. At the same time, the film's concluding voice-over of optimistic moral reassurance is a kind of Hollywood ending and constitutes, as several of my students note, a form of concluding, self-reflexive parody on Allen's part. By resuscitating the voice of the deceased philosopher, a suicide who was the object of one of Cliff's failed documentaries, Allen exploits and transcends the art form itself, while continuing his balance between forces of light and dark.

Moreover, the distinction the film establishes between the interior fictional Allen character, Cliff, and Woody Allen the creative director also demands consideration. The distinction emphasizes another important artistic creation of Woody Allen, namely, his public persona. In a sense, there is no real Woody Allen in that he has become so thoroughly identified with and indistinguishable from his public image, an image darkened by the scandals in his personal life. The public persona of Woody Allen now seems even more powerful and tangible since these controversial events. The ubiquity of this persona and the public's various associations with it are part of Allen's artistry.

However, we still know enough of Woody Allen's origins to discern important parallels between Woody the public figure and the Woody who was born and grew up in Flatbush, Brooklyn. It is a very American story of success, transformation, and loss with deep roots in our national history and culture. Allen's master narrative of transformation and invented identity appears in one guise or another with Zelig-like regularity in all of his films since *Play It Again, Sam*. In these films, he has understood how the experiences of loss, alienation, and uncertainty occur concomitantly with the joy, excitement, and anticipation of individual and cultural renewal. Perhaps it can be argued that his films achieve a unique American quality in their successful synthesis and balance, not only of the comedic and the dramatic, but also of the contending forces of loss and regeneration. His exploration of these themes has matured steadily into an important cultural critique of American values and institutions. At least since *Play It Again, Sam,* he has been involved in a reconsideration of aspects of American character ranging from his portrayal of the American hero in *Play It Again, Sam,* to his parody of the American dream in *Zelig* and *The Purple Rose of Cairo,* to his examination of contemporary sexual mores and family relationships in *Annie Hall* and *Hannah and Her Sisters,* to the dramatization of dilemmas of contemporary ethics and belief in *Manhattan* and *Crimes and Misdemeanors.* Few American artists of the past 20 years have surpassed his influence on their particular art form or exceeded his impact on American culture. Partly because he insists on his right to stretch himself as a director, Allen has produced a major body of work that continues to grow and mature. Having the courage to risk failure, he has achieved artistic success and stands, as Vincent Canby says, as one of our greatest modern film directors.

Notes

1. Mary Erler, "Morality? Don't Ask" in "Woody Allen Counts the Wages of Sin," *New York Times,* Sunday, October 15, 1989, Arts and Leisure, p. 16.

2. Eugene B. Borowitz, "Heeding Ecclesiastes, At Long Last" in "Woody Allen Counts the Wages of Sin," *New York Times,* Sunday, October 15, 1989, Arts and Leisure, p. 16.

3. See Herman Melville, "Hawthorne and His Mosses" (1850) in *Moby Dick,* ed. Harrison Hayford and Hershel Parker (New York: Norton, 1967), p. 547, for the origins of this phrase.

4. Douglas Brode, *Woody Allen: His Films and Career,* 2nd ed. (Secaucus, N.J.: Citadel, 1987), p. 132.

5. Woody Allen, *Hannah and Her Sisters* (New York: Vintage, 1987), p. 131.

6. Ibid., p. 144.

7. Natalie Gittelson, "The Maturing of Woody Allen," *New York Times Magazine,* April 22, 1979, p. 106.

8. Ibid., p. 107.

9. Ibid., p. 102.

10. Pauline Kael, "What's Wrong with This Picture?" "The Current Cinema," *New Yorker,* October 31, 1988, p. 81. See also, e.g., Kael's review of Allen's "Oedipus Wrecks" in *New York Stories,* in "Two-Base Hit," *New Yorker,* March 20, 1989, p. 95: "This is Woody Allen's kind of comedy – the situation harks back to his earlier, funnier films, and the audience is grateful. But what was once peppy and slobby-spirited has become almost oppressively schematic.... It just doesn't have

the organic untidiness that was part of Woody Allen's humor. Even his jokes are clean now, and his malice has been airbrushed out. He can't really revive the kind of comedy he used to do."

11. Tom Shales, "Woody: The First Fifty Years," *Esquire,* April 1987, p. 95.

12. Woody Allen, "Through a Life Darkly," review of *The Magic Lantern: An Autobiography* by Ingmar Bergman, in *New York Times,* Sunday, September 18, 1988, Book Review, p. 30.

13. Ibid.

14. Ibid.

15. Ibid.

16. Woody Allen, *Manhattan* in *Four Films of Woody Allen* (New York: Random House, 1982), p. 201.

17. See Mark Twain, *The Adventures of Huckleberry Finn,* eds. Walter Blair and Victor Fischer, Mark Twain Library Edition (Berkeley and Los Angeles: University of California Press, 1985), p. 271. For a discussion of this issue of conscience and heart and quotation marks in *Huckleberry Finn,* see Henry Nash Smith, *Mark Twain: The Development of a Writer* (New York: Atheneum, 1967), pp. 113–37.

Filmography

What's New, Pussycat?
Screenplay: Woody Allen
Director: Clive Donner
Director of photography: Jean Badel
Editing: Fergus McDonell
Music: Burt Bacharach
Producer: Charles K. Feldman
Production company: Famous Artists
Cast: Peter Sellers, Peter O'Toole, Romy Schneider, Capucine, Paula Prentiss, Woody Allen, Ursula Andress, Edra Gale, Chaterine Schaake, Jess Hahn, Eleanor Hirt, Nicole Karen, Jean Paredes, Michel Subor, Jacqueline Fogt, Robert Rollis, Daniel Emilfork, Louis Falavigni, Jacques Balutin, Annette Poivre, Sabine Sun, Jean Yves Autrey, Pascal Wolf, Nadine Papin, Tanya Lopert, Colin Drake, Norbert Terry, F. Medard, Gordon Felio, Louise Lasser, Richard Saint-Bris, Françoise Hardy, Douking
Running time: 106 min

What's Up, Tiger Lily?
Screenplay: Hideo Ando (original); Woody Allen, Frank Buxton, Len Maxwell, Louise Lasser, Mickey Rose, Julie Bennett, Bryna Wilson (re-release)
Director: Senkichi Taniguchi (original); Woody Allen (re-release)
Director of photography: Kazuo Yamada (original)
Editing: Richard Krown (re-release)
Music: The Lovin' Spoonful (re-release)
Producer: Tomoyuki Tanaka (original); Ben Shapiro (re-release conception)
Production company: Toho (original)

Cast: Tatsuya Mihashi, Mie Hama, Akiko Wakayabayashi, Tadao Nakamaru, Susumu Kurobe (original); Woody Allen, Frank Buxton, Len Maxwell, Louise Lasser, Mickey Rose, Julie Bennett, Bryna Wilson (dubbed in re-release)
Running time: 79 min

1967

Casino Royale
Screenplay: Wolf Mankowitz, John Law, Michael Sayers, suggested by novel by Ian Fleming
Directors: John Huston, Kenneth Hughes, Val Guest, Robert Parrish, Joseph McGrath
Director of photography: Jack Hildyard
Editing: Bill Lenny
Music: Burt Bacharach
Producers: Charles K. Feldman, Jerry Bresler
Production company/Distributor: Famous Artists/Columbia
Cast: Peter Sellers, Ursula Andress, David Niven, Orson Welles, Janna Pettet, Deborah Kerr, Daliah Lavi, Woody Allen, William Holden, Charles Boyer, John Huston, Kurt Kaznar, George Raft, Jean-Paul Belmondo, Terence Cooper, Barbara Bouchet, Angela Scoular, Gabriella Licudi, Tracey Crisp, Jacky Bisset, Anna Quayle, Derek Nimmo, Ronnie Corbett, Colin Gordon, Bernard Cribbens, Tracy Reed, Duncan Macrae, Graham Stark, Richard Wattis, Percy Herbert
Running time: 131 min

1969

Don't Drink the Water
Screenplay: R. S. Allen, Harvey Bullock, after play by Woody Allen
Director: Howard Morris
Director of photography: Harvey Genkins
Editing: Ralph Rosenblum
Music: Pat Williams
Producer: Charles Joffe
Cast: Jackie Gleason, Estelle Parsons, Ted Bessell, Joan Delaney, Richard Libertini, Michael Constantine, Avery Schreiber, Howard St. John, Danny Mehan, Pierre Olaf, Phil Leeds, Mark Gordon, Dwayne Early, Joan Murphy, Martin Danzig, Rene Constantineau, Howard Morris
Running time/Rating: 98 min, G

Take the Money and Run
Screenplay: Woody Allen, Mickey Rose
Director: Woody Allen
Director of photography: Lester Shorr
Editing: Paul Jordan, Ron Kalish
Music: Marvin Hamlisch
Producer: Charles H. Joffe

Production company: Palomar
Cast: Woody Allen, Janet Margolin, Marcel Hillaire, Jacqueline Hyde, Lonnie Chapman, Jan Merlin, James Anderson, Howard Storm, Mark Gordon, Micil Murphy, Minnow Moskowitz, Nate Jacobson, Grace Bauer, Ethel Sokolow, Henry Leff, Don Frazier, Mike O'Dowd, Jackson Beck, Louise Lasser
Running time/Rating: 85 min, M

1971

Bananas
Screenplay: Woody Allen, Mickey Rose
Director: Woody Allen
Director of photography: Andrew M. Costikyan
Editing: Ron Kalish
Music: Marvin Hamlisch
Producer: Jack Grossberg
Production company: Rollins–Joffe
Cast: Woody Allen, Louise Lasser, Carlos Montalban, Natividad Abascal, Jacobo Morales, Miguel Suarez, David Ortiz, Rene Enriquez, Jack Axelrod, Howard Cosell, Roger Grimsby, Don Dunphy, Charlotte Rae, Stanley Ackerman, Dan Frazer, Martha Greenhouse, Axel Anderson, Tigre Perez, Baron de Beer, Arthur Hughes, John Braden, Ted Chapman, Dorthi Fox, Dagne Crane, Ed Barth, Nicholas Saunders, Conrad Bain, Eulogio Peraza, Norman Evans, Robert O'Connel, Robert Dudley, Marilyn Hengst, Ed Crowley, Beeson Carroll, Allen Garfield, Princess Fatosh, Dick Callinan, Hy Anzel
Running time/Rating: 81 min, PG

1972

Play It Again, Sam
Screenplay: Woody Allen, after his play
Director: Herbert Ross
Director of photography: Owen Roizman
Editing: Marion Rothman
Music: Billy Goldenberg
Producer: Arthur P. Jacobs
Distributor: Paramount
Cast: Woody Allen, Diane Keaton, Tony Roberts, Jerry Lacy, Susan Anspach, Jennifer Salt, Joy Bang, Viva, Suzanne Zenor, Diana Davile, Mari Fletcher, Michael Green, Ted Markland
Running time/Rating: 85 min, PG

Everything You Always Wanted to Know About Sex* (*but were afraid to ask)
Screenplay: Woody Allen, after book by David Reuben
Director: Woody Allen
Director of photography: David M. Walsh

Editing: Eric Albertson
Music: Mundel Lowe
Producer: Charles H. Joffe
Distributor: United Artists
Cast: Woody Allen, John Carradine, Lou Jacobi, Louise Lasser, Anthony Quayle, Tony Randall, Lynn Redgrave, Burt Reynolds, Gene Wilder, Jack Barry, Erin Fleming, Elaine Giftos, Toni Holt, Robert Q. Miller, Regis Philbin, Titos Vandis, Stanley Adams, Oscar Beregi, Alan Caillou, Dort Clark, Geoffrey Holder, Jay Robinson, Ref Sanchez, Don Chuy, Tom Mack, Baruch Lumet, Robert Walden, H. E. West
Running time/Rating: 87 min, R

1973

Sleeper
Screenplay: Woody Allen, Marshall Brickman
Director: Woody Allen
Editing: Ralph Rosenblum
Director of photography: David M. Walsh
Music: Woody Allen, Preservation Hall Jazz Band, New Orleans Funeral Ragtime Orchestra
Producer: Jack Grossberg
Production company: Rollins–Joffe
Cast: Woody Allen, Diane Keaton, John Beck, Mary Gregory, Don Keefer, John McLiam, Bartlett Robinson, Chris Forbes, Marya Small, Peter Hobbs, Susan Miller, Lou Picetti, Jessica Rains, Brian Avery, Spencer Milligan, Stanley Ross
Running time/Rating: 88 min, PG

1975

Love and Death
Screenplay: Woody Allen
Director: Woody Allen
Director of photography: Ghislain Cloquet
Editing: Ralph Rosenblum, Ron Kalish
Music: S. Prokofiev
Producer: Charles H. Joffe
Production company: Rollins–Joffe
Cast: Woody Allen, Diane Keaton, Georges Adet, Frank Adu, Edmond Ardisson, Feodor Atkine, Albert Augier, Yves Barsaco, Lloyd Battista, Jack Berard, Eva Bertrand, George Birt, Yves Brainville, Gerard Buhr, Brian Coburn, Henri Coutet, Patricia Crown, Henry Czarniak, Despo Diamantidou, Sandor Eles, Luce Fabiole, Florian, Jacqueline Fogt, Sol L. Frieder, Olga Georges-Picot, Harold Gould, Harry Hankin, Jessica Harper, Tony Jan, Tutte Lemkow, Jack Lenoir, Leib Lensky, Ann Lonnberg, Roger Lumont, Alfred Lutter III, Ed Marcus, Jacques Maury, Narcissa McKinley, Aubrey Morris, Denise Peron, Beth Porter, Alan Rossett, Shimen Ruskin,

Persival Russel, Chris Sanders, Zvee Scooler, C. A. R. Smith, Fred Smith, Bernard Taylor, Clemenet Thierry, Alan Tilvern, James Tolkan, Helene Vallier, Howard Vernon, Glenn Williams, Jacob Witkin
Running time/Rating: 85 min, PG Comedy

1976

The Front

Screenplay: Walter Bernstein
Director: Martin Ritt
Director of photography: Michael Chapman
Editing: Sidney Levin
Music: David Grusin
Producer: Martin Ritt
Production company/Distributor: Ritt–Rollins–Joffe/Columbia
Cast: Woody Allen, Zero Mostel, Herschel Bernardi, Michael Murphy, Andrea Marcovicci, Remak Ramsay, Marvin Lichterman, Lloyd Gough, David Margulies, Joshua Shelley, Norman Rose, Charles Kimbrough, M. Josef Sommer, Danny Aiello, Georgann Johnson, Scott McKay, David Clarke, J. W. Klein, John Bentley, Julie Garfield, Murray Moston, McIntyre Dixon, Rudolph Wilrich, Burt Bogert, Joey Faye, Marilyn Sokol, John J. Slater, Renee Paris, Joan Porter, Andrew Bernstein, Jacob Bernstein, Matthew Tobin, Marilyn Persky, Sam McMurray, Joe Jamrog, Michael Miller, Jack Davidson, Donald Symington, Patrick McNamara
Running time/Rating: 94 min, R

1977

Woody Allen: An American Comedy

Director/Producer: Harold Mantell
Distributor: Films for the Humanities, Inc.
Narrator: Woody Allen

Annie Hall

Screenplay: Woody Allen, Marshall Brickman
Director: Woody Allen
Director of photography: Gordon Willis
Editing: Ralph Rosenblum
Producer: Charles H. Joffe
Executive producer: Robert Greenhut
Production company/Distributor: Rollins–Joffe/United Artists
Cast: Woody Allen, Diane Keaton, Tony Roberts, Carol Kane, Paul Simon, Shelley Duvall, Janet Margolin, Colleen Dewhurst, Christopher Walken, Donald Symington, Helen Ludlam, Mordecai Lawner, Joan Newman, Jonathan Munk, Ruth Volner, Martin Rosenblatt, Hy Ansel, Rashel Novikoff, Russell Horton, Marshall McLuhan, Christine Jones, Mary Boylan, Wendy Girard, John Doumanian, Bob Maroff, Rick

135

Petrucelli, Lee Callahan, Chris Gampel, Dick Cavett, John Glover, Bernie Styles, Johnny Haymer, Ved Bandhu, John Dennis, Johnston, Lauri Bird, Jim McKrell, Jeff Goldblum, William Callaway, Roger Newman, Alan Landers, Jean Sarah Frost, Vince O'Brien, Humphrey Davis, Veronica Radburn, Robin Mary Paris, Charles Levin, Wayne Carson, Michael Karm, Petronia Johnson, Shaun Casey, Ticardo Bertoni, Michael Aronin, Lou Picetti, Loretta Tupper, James Burge, Shelly Hack, Albert Ottenheimer, Paula Trueman, Beverly D'Angelo, Tracey Walter, David Wier, Keith Dentice, Susan Mellinger, Hamit Perezic, James Balter, Eric Gould, Amy Levitan, Gary Allen, Frank Vohs, Sybil Bowan, Margaretta Warwick, Lucy Lee Flippen, Gary Muledeer, Sigourney Weaver, Walter Bernstein, Artie Butler
Running time/Rating: 93 min, PG

1978

Interiors
Screenplay: Woody Allen
Director: Woody Allen
Director of photography: Gordon Willis
Editing: Ralph Rosenblum
Producer: Charles H. Joffe
Executive producer: Robert Greenhut
Production company/Distributor: Rollins–Joffe/United Artists
Cast: Kristen Griffith, Marybeth Hurt, Richard Jordan, Diane Keaton, E. G. Marshall, Geraldine Page, Maureen Stapleton, Sam Waterston, Missy Hope, Kerry Duffy, Nancy Collins, Penny Gaston, Roger Morden, Henderson Forsythe
Running time/Rating: 93 min, PG

1979

Manhattan
Screenplay: Woody Allen, Marshall Brickman
Director: Woody Allen
Director of photography: Gordon Willis
Editing: Susan E. Morse
Music: George Gershwin
Producer: Charles H. Joffe
Executive producer: Robert Greenhut
Production company/Distributor: Rollins–Joffe/United Artists
Cast: Woody Allen, Diane Keaton, Michael Murphy, Mariel Hemingway, Meryl Streep, Anne Byrne, Karen Ludwig, Michael O'Donoghue, Victor Truro, Tisa Farrow, Helen Hanft, Bella Abzug, Gary Weis, Kenny Vance, Charles Levin, Karen Allen, David Rasche, Damion Sheller, Wallace Shawn, Mark Linn Baker, Frances Conroy, Bill Anthony, John Doumanian, Ray Serra
Running time/Rating: 96 min, R

Stardust Memories
Screenplay: Woody Allen
Director: Woody Allen
Director of photography: Gordon Willis
Editing: Susan E. Morse
Producer: Robert Greenhut
Executive producers: Jack Rollins, Charles H. Joffe
Production company/Distributor: Rollins–Joffe/United Artists
Cast: Woody Allen, Charlotte Rampling, Jessica Harper, Marie-Christine Barrault, Tony Roberts, Daniel Stern, Amy Wright, Helen Hanft, John Rothman, Anne DeSalvo, Joan Neuman, Ken Chapin, Leonardo Cimino, Eli Mintz, Bob Maroff, Gebrielle Strasun, David Lipman, Robert Munk, Jagui Safra, Sraon Stone, Andy Albeck, Robert Friedman, Douglas Ireland, Jack Rollins, Howard Kissel, Max Leavitt, Renee Lippin, Sol Lomita, Irving Metzman, Dorothy Leon, Roy Brocksmith, Simon Newey, Victoria Zussin, Frances Pole, Bill Anthony, Filomena Spagnuolo, Ruth Rugoff, Martha Whitehead, Judith Roberts, Barry Weiss, Robin Ruinsky, Adrian Richards, Dominick Petrolino, Sharon Brous, Michael Zannella, Doris Dugan Slater, Michael Goldstein, Niel Napolitan, Stanley Ackerman, Noel Behn, Candy Loving, Denice Danon, Sally Demay, Tom Dennis, Edward Kotkin, Laura Delano, Lisa Friendman, Brent Spiner, Gardenia Cole, Maurice Shrog, Larry Roberts Carr, Brian Zoldessy, Melissa Slade, Paula Raflo, Jordan Derwin, Tony Azito, Marc Murray, Helen Hale, Carl Dorn, Victoria Page, Bert Michaels, Deborah Johnson, Benjamin Rayson, Mary Mims, Charles Lowe, Marie Lane, Gustave Tassell, Marina Schiano, Dimitri Vassilopoulos, Judith Crist, Carmin Mastrin, Sylvia Davis, Joseph Summo, Victor Truro, Irwin Keyes, Bonnie Hellman, Patrick Daly, Joe Pagano, Wayne Maxwell, Ann Freeman, Bob Miranti, Cindy Gibb, Manuella Machado, Judith Cohen, Madeline Moroff, Maureen P. Levins, E. Brian Dean, Marvin Peisner, Robert Tennenhouse, Leslie Smith, Samuel Chodorov, Philip Lenkowsky, Vanina Holasek, Michel Touchard, Kanny Vance, Iryn Steinfink, Frank Modell, Anne Korzen, Eric Van Valkenburg, Susan Ginsburg, Ostaro, Wade Barnes, Garbiel Barre, Charles Riggs III, Geoffrey Riggs, Martha Sherrill, Ann Risley, Jade Bari, Marc Geller, Daniel Friedman, James Otis, Judy Goldner, Rebeccas Wright, Perry Gewertz, Larry Fishman, Liz Albrecht, Sloane Bosniak, James Harter, Henry House, Largo Woodruff, Jerry Tov Greenberg, Mohammid Nabi Kiani, Alice Spivak, Armin Shimerman, Edith Grossman, Jacqueline French, John Doumanian, Jack Hollander
Running time/Rating: 89, PG

A Midsummer Night's Sex Comedy
Screenplay: Woody Allen
Director: Woody Allen
Director of photography: Gordon Willis

Editing: Susan E. Morse
Producer: Robert Greenhut
Executive producer: Charles H. Joffe
Production company/Distributor: Rollins–Joffe/Orion
Cast: Woody Allen, José Ferrer, Mia Farrow, Julie Hagerty, Tony Roberts, Mary Steenburgen
Running time/Rating: 94 min, PG

1983

Zelig
Screenplay: Woody Allen
Director: Woody Allen
Director of photography: Gordon Willis
Editing: Susan E. Morse
Producer: Robert Greenhut
Executive producer: Charles H. Joffe
Production company/Distributor: Rollins–Joffe/Orion
Cast: Woody Allen, Mia Farrow, Ellen Garrison, Mary Louise Wilson, Stephanie Farrow, John Doumanian, Erma Campbell, Jean Towbridge, Deborah Rush
Contemporary interviews: Susan Sontag, Irving Howe, Saul Bellow, Bricktop, Dr. Bruno Bettelheim, Prof. John Morton Blum
Announcers: Ed Herlihy, Dwight Weist, Gordon Gould, Windy Craig, Jurgen Kuehn
Narration: Patrick Horgan
Running time/Rating: 79 min, PG

1984

Broadway Danny Rose
Screenplay: Woody Allen
Director: Woody Allen
Director of photography: Gordon Willis
Editing: Susan E. Morse
Producer: Robert Greenhut
Production company/Distributor: Rollins–Joffe/Orion
Cast: Woody Allen, Mia Farrow, Nick Apollo Forte, Corbett Monica, Howard Storm, Morty Gunty, Sandy Baron, Will Jordan, Jackie Gayle, Jack Rollins, Milton Berle, Howard Cosell, Joe Franklin, Craig Vanderburgh, Hugh Reynolds, Paul Greco, Frank Renzulli, Edwin Bordo, Gina DeAngelis, Gloria Parker, Bob Rollins, Etta Rollins, John Doumanian, Leo Steiner
Running time/Rating: 85 min, PG

1985

The Purple Rose of Cairo
Screenplay: Woody Allen
Director: Woody Allen

Director of photography: Gordon Willis
Editing: Susan E. Morse
Producer: Robert Greenhut
Production company/Distributor: Rollins–Joffe/Orion
Cast: Mia Farrow, Jeff Daniels, Danny Aiello, Dianne Wiest, Edward Herrmann, Van Johnson, Irving Metzman, Stephanie Farrow, David Kiserman, John Wood, Deborah Rush, Zoe Caldwell, Eugene Anthony, Ebb Miller, Karen Akers, Annie Joe Edwards, Milo O'Shea, Dianne Wiest, Helen Hanft
Running time/Rating: 81 min, PG

1986

Hannah and Her Sisters
Screenplay: Woody Allen
Director: Woody Allen
Director of photography: Carlo di Palma
Editing: Susan E. Morse
Producer: Robert Greenhut
Production company/Distributor: Rollins–Joffe/Orion
Cast: Barbara Hershey, Carrie Fisher, Michael Caine, Mia Farrow, Dianne Wiest, Maureen O'Sullivan, Lloyd Nolan, Max Von Sydow, Woody Allen, Tony Roberts, Sam Waterston, Lewis Black, Julia Louis-Dreyfus, Christian Clemenson, Julie Kavner, J. T. Walsh, John Turturro, Rusty Magee, Allen Decheser, Artie Decheser, Ira Wheeler, Richard Jenkins, Tracy Kennedy, Fred Melamed, Benno Schmidt, Joanna Gleason, Maria Chiara, Daniel Stern, Stephen Defluiter, The 39 Steps, Bobby Short, Rob Scott, Beverly Peer, Daisy Previn, Moses Farrow, Paul Bates, Carrotte, Mary Pappas, Bernie Leighton, Ken Costigan, Helen Miller, Leo Postrel, Susan Gordon-Clark, William Sturgis, Daniel Haber, Verna O. Hobson, John Doumanian, Fletcher Previn, Irwin Tenebaum, Amy Greenhill, Dickson Shaw, Marje Sheridan, Ivan Kronenfeld
Running time/Rating: 106 min, PG-13

1987

September
Screenplay: Woody Allen
Director: Woody Allen
Director of photography: Carlo di Palma
Editing: Susan E. Morse
Producer: Robert Greenhut
Production company/Distributor: Rollins–Joffe/Orion
Cast: Denholm Elliott, Mia Farrow, Elaine Stritch, Jack Warden, Sam Waterston, Dianne Wiest, Ira Wheeler, Jane Cecil, Rosemary Murphy
Running time/Rating: 82 min, PG

Radio Days
Screenplay: Woody Allen
Director: Woody Allen
Director of photography: Carlo di Palma
Editing: Susan E. Morse
Producer: Robert Greenhut
Production company/Distributor: Rollins–Joffe/Orion
Cast: Mia Farrow, Seth Green, Julie Kavner, Diane Keaton, Tony Roberts, Danny Aiello, Jeff Daniels, Josh Mostel, Dianne Wiest, Wallace Shawn, Michael Tucker, Jay Newman, Hy Anzell, Kenneth Mars, Tito Puente, Kitty Carlisle Hart
Running time/Rating: 91 min, PG

1988

Another Woman
Screenplay: Woody Allen
Director: Woody Allen
Director of photography: Sven Nykvist
Editing: Susan E. Morse
Producer: Robert Greenhut
Production company/Distributor: Rollins–Joffe/Orion
Cast: Gena Rowlands, Mia Farrow, Ian Holm, Blythe Danner, Martha Plimpton, John Houseman, Sandy Dennis, Gene Hackman, Betty Buckley, David Ogden Stiers, Philip Bosco, Harris Yulin, Frances Conroy
Running time/Rating: 84 min, PG

1989

Oedipus Wrecks (short film in omnibus New York Stories**)**
Screenplay: Woody Allen
Director: Woody Allen
Director of photography: Sven Nykvist
Editing: Susan E. Morse
Producer: Robert Greenhut
Production company/Distributor: Rollins–Joffe/Orion & Greenhut for Touchstone Pictures
Cast: Woody Allen, Mia Farrow, Mae Questel, Julie Kavner, Marvin Chatinover
Running time: 45 min (this short only)

Crimes and Misdemeanors
Screenplay: Woody Allen
Director: Woody Allen
Director of photography: Sven Nykvist
Editing: Susan E. Morse
Producer: Robert Greenhut
Production company/Distributor: Rollins–Joffe/Orion
Cast: Caroline Aaron, Alan Alda, Woody Allen, Claire Bloom, Mia Farrow, Joanna

140

Gleason, Anjelica Huston, Martin Landau, Jenny Nichols, Jerry Orbach, Sam Waterston
Running time/Rating: 104 min, PG-13

1991

Alice
Screenplay: Woody Allen
Director: Woody Allen
Director of photography: Carlo di Palma
Editing: Susan E. Morse
Producer: Robert Greenhut
Production company/Distributor: Rollins–Joffe/Orion
Cast: Mia Farrow, William Hurt, Joe Mantegna, Keye Luke, Alec Baldwin, Blythe Danner, Judy Davis, Bernadette Peters, Cybill Shepherd, Gwen Verdon
Running time/Rating: 106 min, PG-13

1992

Scenes from a Mall
Screenplay: Roger L. Simon, Paul Mazursky
Director: Paul Mazursky
Director of photography: Fred Murphy
Editing: Stuart Pappe
Producer: Paul Mazursky
Production company/Distributor: A Buena Vista Release of a Touchstone Pictures Presentation in association with Silver Screen Partner IV of a Paul Mazursky production
Cast: Bette Midler, Woody Allen, Bill Irwin, Daren Firestone, Rebecca Nickels, Paul Mazursky
Running time/Rating: 87 min, R

Additional films cited

Casablanca, dir. Michael Curtiz (Warner Bros., U.S., 1942)
Citizen Kane, dir. Orson Welles (RKO, U.S., 1941)
Discreet Charm of the Bourgeoisie, The (Le Charme discret de la bourgeoisie), dir. Luis Buñuel (Greenwich, France, 1972)
Goodbye Girl, The, dir. Herbert Ross (Warner Bros., U.S., 1977)
Great Dictator, The, dir. Charles Chaplin (United Artists, U.S., 1940)
Maltese Falcon, The, dir. John Huston (Warner Bros., U.S., 1941)
Marnie, dir. Alfred Hitchcock (Universal, U.S., 1964)
Modern Times, dir. Charles Chaplin (Chaplin, U.S., 1936)
Monsieur Verdoux, dir. Charles Chaplin (Chaplin, U.S., 1947)
Portnoy's Complaint, dir. Ernest Lehman (Warner Bros., U.S., 1972)
Psycho, dir. Alfred Hitchcock (Paramount, U.S., 1960)
Saturday Night Fever, dir. John Badham (Paramount, U.S., 1977)

Seven Per Cent Solution, The, dir. Herbert Ross (Universal, U.S., 1976)
Sherlock Junior, dir. Buster Keaton (Metro/Keaton, U.S., 1924)
Top Hat, dir. Mark Sandrich (RKO, U.S., 1935)
Turning Point, The, dir. Herbert Ross (Paramount, U.S., 1977)
Wild Strawberries (Smultronstället), dir. Ingmar Bergman (Svensk Film Industry, Sweden, 1957)
Wizard of Oz, The, dir. Victor Fleming (MGM, U.S., 1939)

Index

Landau, Martin, 117
language, 28, 35–7, 46–7, 83
Lax, Eric, 4, 11, 70, 87, 89, 90
Lee, Spike, 1
lesbianism, 48, 62, 66
Love and Death, 90

Macbeth, 77
McCann, Graham, 34, 35, 46, 59, 72, 98, 109n4
McCarthy, Mary, 98
McCartney, Paul, 64
McLuhan, Marshall, 34–5
Madame Bovary, 71
Magic Lantern, The, 114
Maltese Falcon, The, 17–18
"Man of the Crowd," 73
Manhattan, 5, 11, 16, 43–69, 73–4, 77–8, 89, 91–3, 97–8, 114–17, 119, 125, 128
Marnie, 9
Marx Bros., 108
Marxism, 125
mass man, 73–4
media, 4, 74–6, 78, 87
Melville, Herman, 43
methodology, 7
Metz, Christian, 10, 17
Midsummer Night's Sex Comedy, A, 59, 89
mimesis, 26–7
Mitchell, Juliet, 14
Modern Times, 76
Monsieur Verdoux, 76
Moore, Gary, 2
"Most Prevalent Form of Degradation in Erotic Life," 24n17
Munich, 73
Murphy, Michael, 47
Museum of Modern Art, 61
Mussolini, Benito, 124

narcissism, 41, 53, 63, 124, 125
narrative, 8–9, 25–8, 35–6, 38, 118, 126
narrative discourse, 28–42, 58–60, 66, 92, 101
Nazis, 72–4
New York City, 9
Nicholson, Jack, 61
Nietzsche, Friedrich, 100
Nolan, Lloyd, 95

Oedipal theory, 14, 25
Old Testament, 123
Orbach, Jerry, 118
O'Sullivan, Maureen, 95

Paar, Jack, 2
Page, Geraldine, 78

Passover, 111, 123, 125
photography, 76
Play It Again, Sam, 2, 5, 11, 12–23, 42, 58, 72, 77, 87, 108, 115–18, 127–8
Poe, Edgar Allan, 73, 123
Pogel, Nancy, 11, 34
Porter, Cole, 85
Portnoy's Complaint, 39
pre-Oedipal and prelinguistic theory, 14
presence, and absence, 17
propaganda, 10, 74, 76
psychoanalysis, 7, 9, 19–20, 25, 29, 33, 41, 63
Purple Rose of Cairo, The, 6, 11, 27, 70–88, 90, 128

Queens, N.Y., 52

Radio Days, 11, 111
Rafferty, Terrence, 1
reality, 70–1, 75, 77, 83–4
Reiner, Rob, 1
repression, 25, 31
"Rhapsody in Blue," 43–4, 69
Rich, Frank, 69n2
Roberts, Tony, 19, 26, 101
Rogers, Ginger, 85
Rollins, Jack, 2
Rose, Jacqueline, 14
Rose, Lloyd, 87
Ross, Herb, 12–13
Roth, Philip, 10–11, 18–19, 39
Rothman, William, 12
Russian Tea Room, 62

Safer, Morley, 4
Sahl, Mort, 2
"schlemiel" figure, 3, 30, 72, 89
Schubert, Franz, 117
Scope-screen, 46–60, 115, 119
semiotics, 7, 13, 15, 19, 25
September, 11, 78, 87, 113
Seven Per Cent Solution, The, 12
sexism, 29–30
"sexts," 9
sexual revolution, 3, 19, 115
Shakespeare, William, 77, 123
Shales, Tom, 113–14
Sherlock Junior, 71
Side Effects, 3
signifying process, 7, 12–15, 25, 36, 54
Silverman, Kaja, 10, 13, 16–17
Sinatra, Frank, 33
Smith, Henry Nash, 10, 129n17
"Someone to Watch Over Me," 51–2
"somewhere i have never travelled,gladly beyond," 103